THE FAITH OF THE UNBELIEVER

The content of the Christian faith is unchanging but its presentation must continually be adapted to the culture and beliefs of contemporary society. Martin Robinson has made an invaluable contribution to our understanding of how our world thinks. This book is vital reading for all who wish to relate an unchanging word to a changing world.

— *Rev Clive Calver*
President, World Relief

A book that explodes myths, informs intelligently and is full of perspective and insight.

— *Gerald Coates*
Director, Pioneer

The Faith
of the
Unbeliever

MARTIN ROBINSON

**MONARCH
BOOKS**

Mill Hill, London & Grand Rapids, Michigan

Published by Monarch Books,
Concorde House, Grenville Place,
Mill Hill, London, NW7 3SA.
First published in the UK in 1994. Reprinted 1997.
New edition 2001.

Published in the USA by Monarch Books 2001.

Distributed by:
UK: STL, PO Box 300, Kingstown Broadway, Carlisle,
Cumbria CA3 0QS;
USA: Kregel Publications, PO Box 2607
Grand Rapids, Michigan 49501.

ISBN 1 85424 568 6 (UK)
ISBN 0 8254 6043 3 (USA)

Published in conjunction with Bible Society.
Bible Society's vision is to equip the people of God
with the resources to make the Bible accessible and
relevant to today's world. Bible Society can be
contacted at Stonehill Green, Westlea,
Swindon SN5 7DG.

British Library Cataloguing-in-Publication Data
A catalogue record for this book is available
from the British Library.

Book design and production for the publishers by
Bookprint Creative Services
P.O. Box 827, BN21 3YJ, England
Printed in Great Britain.

CONTENTS

INTRODUCTION TO THE NEW EDITION

The main ideas contained in *The Faith of the Unbeliever* were fashioned in the early 1990s. The references in the main text to contemporary events reflect the period in which the text was written. At the time the title was chosen, some at least had to ponder hard whether unbelief could be a kind of faith. Today few would doubt that there is a faith commitment in the stand of the atheist. That shift reflects the increasing importance of post-modernity as a critique of modernity.

On re-reading *The Faith of the Unbeliever*, I have realised that the distinction between modernity and post-modernity is described but not summarised. I thought that it might be helpful to some if I were to include such a summary as a brief introductory essay in this second edition of the book.

The author Alvin Toffler was the first to coin the phrase 'Future Shock'. By this he meant that the process of change, particularly technological change, has accelerated in recent years to such an extent that we no longer have time to absorb one set of changes before the next set engulfs us. The impact on our culture of such change is profound and far reaching.

Ever since the Western world began to emerge as the dominant economic and military power in the world, expressed particularly through empire and colonialisation, the process of globalisation has gradually extended so that there has come an increasing sense of the prevailing presence of one world culture. The effects of globalisation can perhaps be seen more clearly in the realm of youth culture but increasingly its effects are felt by all. The so called primitive 'stone age' tribespeople of Papua New Guinea, who attracted world headlines through the kidnapping of several Western hostages, monitored the effects of their hostage taking through a web site on the internet.

The phenomenon of globalisation reflects very well the impact of modernity so that even though some feel that modernity as a world view is coming to a conclusion its effects are still powerful enough that we need to understand the basic assumptions that have powered its rise.

The condition of modernity

What then is modernity? Put very simply, modernity is the term we use to describe the way the Western world has been for the last few hundred years. Precisely because it is hard for us to discern that which we regard as normality, it has been hard to recognise that the culture of which we are a part has its own belief set. Yet, increasingly, thinkers are coming to acknowledge and identify the powerful assumptions or features that underlie our view of 'normality'.

Six key features of modernity

1. Understanding the world through reason alone   The coming of the modern era, and particularly the philosophical movement which we call the Enlightenment, introduced the claim that we can only know the world through the exercise of reason. The disciplines by which reason might be exercised would differ in various philosophical traditions: for example, the empirical tradition in Britain was rather different to the rationalist tradition of the continent, but the underlying theme of reason was common to both.

It is possible to ask, but how else might we know the world but through reason? That question is understandable but reflects the degree to which we are unconsciously part of modernity. In many cultures in other parts of the world, and certainly in the medieval period prior to modernity, reason and revelation were seen as two parallel ways of knowing the world. In short, there was a claim that some things can only be known by revelation and are simply not knowable by the exercise of reason alone. Inherent in the Christian tradition was the claim that revelation was not lacking in reason, therefore reason and revelation operate in creative tension. Curiously, modernity contains its own hidden revelatory statements. For example, the claim that the world can only be known through the exercise of reason is itself a revelatory statement.

2. The subjective/objective split   Those who wished to emphasise reason still had to recognise that not all things could be known in this way. For example, ethical and religious claims lie beyond the use of reason alone. As the philosopher John Milbank makes clear, ultimately there is a choice to be made between the love of power and the power of love. Reason can be utilised in making such a choice but our will to exercise power or not will certainly play a part. To deal with this apparent difficulty, philosophers such as Kant suggested that the world could be divided into the subjective and objective realms. The material world could be understood as lying in the objective world while religion and ethics belonged in the subjective realm.

Kant had hoped to protect religion and ethics from too close a scrutiny by this device but, over time, the actual effect was rather different. In practice, the separation of reality into the objective and the subjective has produced a situation in which the objective, or public sphere, has been seen as the important area in which the real world operates. The subjective has been come to be seen as the world of opinion which, by implication, is less important.

3. Cause and effect   The move towards a view of the universe as essentially material in its makeup, was accompanied by a view which sees events in the world as capable of being understood in terms of cause and effect. For example, if someone were to have a car accident, the question would be, 'What caused the event?' Speculation and enquiry would want to investigate issues such as the speed of the vehicle, the state of the brakes, the condition of the driver and so on.

What other way of looking at the world might there be? In medieval times, the response of those observing an event might well be to ask, 'What is the moral purpose that underlies the event?'. In much the same way, a Hindu in India might ask, 'What was the state of the karma of those involved?'. The move to a cause and effect means of observing the world tends to remove a sense of there being a moral purpose that lies behind the universe.

4. Facts as value free   Accompanying the idea of the objective arose the idea that objective knowledge leads to the furnishing of hard facts about reality which are themselves value free. The result of this approach suggests that religion must be taught on the basis of known facts with no subjective experiential ingredient. In the past, this has sometimes led to the view in the world of education that religion can only be properly taught by those who do not believe anything and not by those who are believers. There is now much more healthy scepticism that anyone can have access to value-free facts. We all invest some value in the facts that we select as accurate and truthful accounts of our world.

5. The inevitability of progress   The broader attachment to a view of the world as a place which can be known, discovered and understood by the proper exercise of reason, suggested that the power of such an approach leads inevitably to the progress of mankind, essentially towards utopia. Thus, the increase of knowledge, the spread of education and the development of technology would inevitably lead to each successive generation being wealthier, healthier and happier. This kind of view actually amounted to an ideological commitment to progress which found it difficult to take account of the reality of evil as anything other than the denial of reason. The notion that anyone who had received the benefits of education would do anything other than subscribe to the same view of the world as those who had an Enlightenment perspective was largely unthinkable. Such thinking lies behind popular sentiment which says, 'You can't stand in the path of progress.'

6. The rights of the individual   In the Enlightenment framework of thinking, the individual and more particularly the rights of the individual were promoted as carrying considerable value. This contrasted with the earlier medieval framework which had stressed society and the duty of the individual towards society. This can be stated as a tension between rights and responsibilities. In modernity, the duty of society is to uphold the rights of the individual, and the individual has very few responsibilities towards that society. Conversely it could be argued that in a medieval framework the individual had responsibilities or duties towards society and society had correspondingly less duty in terms of upholding the rights of individuals.

Taken together, these six features of modernity have acted as a powerful hidden story which have helped to shape the assumptions that people in the West have used to judge the claims of faith.

The condition of post-modernity

In recent times, writers have spoken of post-modernity without a complete consensus surrounding its meaning. Curiously, we have only really spoken of modernity as a cultural phenomenon once the term post-modernity was coined. One newspaper writer quipped, 'Post-modernity. This term is absolutely meaningless – use it as often as possible.' Despite difficulties with the term we can identify some meaning but it does help if we understand what the difficulties are. A large part of the difficulty surrounds the fact that the term has a slightly different technical meaning depending on whether it is being used in the field of architecture, art, literature, history or philosophy. In very general terms, its present use in the field of philosophy has stemmed from arguments based on linguistic analysis.

What then is post-modernity? There is no complete agreement on what post-modernity actually is. Some see it as a reaction to modernity which eventually modernity will take account of and accommodate. Others take the view that it is a staging post on the way towards something else which at the moment we cannot see. Still others see it as modernity speeded up, a kind of extreme form of modernity. Many believe that post-modernity is the coming reality and that although modernity has not yet collapsed it is in process of so doing. Whether or not we can really agree on the permanence of post-modernity as a new culture defining condition, there is rather more agreement concerning some of its key contours or features.

Four key features of post-modernity

1. The dominance of relativity   One element of apparent continuity with the world of modernity surrounds the issue of relativity. Post-modernity takes the argument of modernity in relation to the subjective sphere where all has only relative value, and has extended that value to the objective sphere as well. More correctly we should say that in a post-modern framework the old divide between the objective and the subjective has been ended in that the subjective realm has been extended so that it now includes the areas that were previously seen as comprising the objective sphere. Everything is now subjective. There is now no such thing as the objective. The subject affects the object to such an extent that all must now be regarded as to some degree falling within a subjective and hence relatively true realm. This new radicalism regarding our ability to know what is true and false is uncompromising in its view of any and all truth claims.

2. *The end of meaning*   From the perspective of post-modernity there are no absolutes precisely because there is no final objective meaning in the universe. The only meaning that one can derive is the meaning that an individual gains through a dynamic interaction with or experience of the world. Meaning is therefore entirely a subjective matter and is individual, transitory, particular and never universal. Some have argued that interaction with the world, or the 'now moment', can be enhanced by means of drugs, sex, religion or indeed a combination of all three.

3. *The rejection of meta-narratives*   In parallel with this tendency comes the declaration that precisely because the world has no ultimate meaning, there is no value in looking for meta-narratives by which to order or explain our understanding of the world. Post-modernity consciously rejects all meta-narratives, beginning with the meta-narrative of modernity and including the meta-narrative which is the Christian story of salvation history.

What are those meta-narratives? In very simple terms the Christian meta-narrative makes the claim that God created the universe, including humanity and that creation fell from perfection due to the eruption of evil. God had a plan to restore his creation and that plan began with the call of Abraham and the subsequent covenant with the people of Israel. The history of Israel culminated in the coming of Jesus, the Messiah, whose life, death, resurrection and ascension marks the centre point of all history from which perspective we can properly understand the universe in which we live. The events surrounding Jesus the Christ are the centre point from which the whole cosmos derives meaning.

The secular meta-narrative with which all Westerners have grown up begins with the assertion that the world came into being by means of a cosmic accident. That accident included the possibility of life and through gradual processes life has emerged from the primeval swamp to become ever more sophisticated. That evolutionary process resulted in mankind assuming an intelligent interaction with his world. Man's first response to his world was to understand through superstition and then through religion. But now, mankind has come of age so that he now realises that God is merely the creation of man's imagination. God now needs to die and give way to the kind of super-man who can control and conquer the universe. Science and technology have given mankind the ability to gain such mastery over the elements, and education is the means for extending knowledge. The end result will be the ending of war, famine, disease and conflict. The inevitable outcome of progress will be the brotherhood of man at which time the kingdom of man will replace the Christian notion of the kingdom of God.

Christians have often found themselves living something of a schizophrenic existence in that a secular world view underpins most of their working, professional lives but on Sundays they believe a different story. The tension is not always conscious but it exists and produces real problems for Christians as they attempt to grapple with a coherent way of explaining the Christian faith to others without simply falling into the trap of saying 'it works for me' which implicitly recognises that Christianity has no value as public truth.

4. The end of history   The rejection of meaning and so of metanarratives also suggests that history itself is not as precise a science as modernity has suggested. Indeed the very act of detecting and telling an historical theme is seen from the perspective of post-modernity as the story of the powerful, the victors and not an objective account at all. However since there is no possibility of an objective account then it follows that there really is no such thing as history. In one sense there is really no past, in terms of a detectable pattern, there is rather only a series of now moments. The past and the future become subsumed in what some have called the perpetual present. The net result of such claims often seems to be the end of hope as much as the end of history.

Earthing the theory

The descriptions of both modernity and post-modernity found above have a rather abstract feel. The reality is that we seldom meet any of these conditions of consciousness in their pure form. In truth, our culture contains a broad mix of both these tendencies. Modernity has not rolled over and died in the face of the critique from post-modernity. There are powerful institutions in our culture, the universities in particular, which have a huge investment in modernity. However, the critique from post-modernity has been and is sufficiently powerful that it cannot be ignored.

At the level of popular culture, post-modernity makes an increasingly large impact, especially in youth culture. The issue of age is an important factor in assessing the relative influences of modernity and post-modernity. There seems to be something of a fulcrum in operation with those who were the 60s generation having been brought up firmly in modernity but being the first generation to experience something of what was to come in post-modernity. In very general terms, we can describe those who are above the age of 50 as bedded in modernity and those under 40 as more influenced by post-modernity. The gulf of understanding between those aged 20 and those aged 70 is correspondingly greater.

The Valleys of South Wales

In terms of the impact of these ideologies, it can sometimes help to feel the difference through story rather than simply to grapple with analysis. A few years ago I met a minister working on a large working class estate in South Wales. The estate was one which had been erected after the Second World War in response to the very poor housing conditions in the town. Those who had moved into the estate in the first decade were immensely proud of this achievement. Here at last was decent housing, with indoor toilets, clean water, good schools, proper medical care and green open spaces. Here it would be possible to build the 'new Jerusalem'.

Fifty years on the cracks in the social experiment are very wide indeed. The children or grandchildren of those who first moved to this area are now unemployed, often using drugs and sometimes involved in the kind of petty crime which supports such drug use.

The churches have not thrived in such a setting. The particular minister that I talked with described the bridges that they were attempting to build with the community. In very general terms they found that the older generation shared the same ethical framework as the Christian community but wanted little to do with the church and its message. In their thinking you did not have to go to church to be a 'good person'. Indeed, the best kind of Christians were those who did good rather than simply sang hymns about it. Religion was a private matter and not up for discussion.

The younger generation, by contrast, shared none of their parents' and grandparents' ethical framework. The knew little of Christian ways of understanding the world but they were very interested indeed to talk about religion. There was a huge gulf of understanding between these two groups – the one formed by modernity the other by post-modernity. Often, the only response of those over 50 years of age was to buy bigger bolts to protect themselves from the ravages of crime.

Milingo of Zambia

Some years ago the Roman Catholic Archbishop of Zambia, a man called Archbishop Milingo, discovered that he had a gift of healing. Naturally, in the context of Africa, his ministry attracted a good deal of attention, to the point where large crowds often gathered to hear him preach and to be prayed for by the Archbishop. His activities caused some concern at the Vatican to the point where he was summoned to Rome to take part in an examination of his beliefs and practices.

Eventually, he was found to be entirely sound in his theology and pastoral practice but the Vatican authorities did not wish to send him back to his Archdiocese. Instead, they kept him in Rome working mainly in poorer parishes. In Rome, many of the poor had long since deserted the Catholic Church, often in favour of spiritists and the like. But when the Archbishop began to preach in these Roman churches, empty churches filled up and astonishing scenes took place.

In some services, those who had been involved in the occult, on hearing the gospel would begin to cry out, in some cases to roll on the floor and generally display signs of demonic possession. This was not a problem to the Archbishop who had seen these manifestation during his African ministry. He would stop preaching, minister to the afflicted and then continue his sermon!

These dramatic scenes were shown on a Channel Four documentary and as I watched them I found that I was moved to the point of tears. Some tears were tears of joy at seeing the poor set free. Some were tears of joy as I marvelled at the amazing sense of humour that God has in reaching into 'darkest Africa' to bring missionary to preach in the shadow of the Vatican. Still others were tears of sadness as I wondered at how the church in Europe has emasculated the gospel message in the face of modernity only to find that an increasing post-modernity has rendered useless the forces of a theology that had sought an accommodation with modernity.

In very recent times Milingo has left Rome and has had an increasingly controversial dialogue with the Unification Church. Part of that dialogue has included his marriage to a Korean woman. This is likely to be the last straw for the Vatican but Milingo's astonishing testimony as a very unusual missionary to the West remains.

In both these stories we see the effects of modernity and of post-modernity. The church has yet to find a meaningful response to either but at least in the context of post-modernity religion is back on the agenda. What matters now is how the church recovers its missionary understanding of itself. A missionary spirituality for the times must be high on the agenda.

Note

The author is indebted to the late Lesslie Newbigin for a lecture containing some of the features of modernity described above.

INTRODUCTION

The age in which we live is often characterised as an age of unbelief. What is meant by such a description is specifically the rejection of belief in matters such as miracles, divine revelation, the realm of the supernatural and the existence of an afterlife lived in heaven. These are all Christian ideas and so unbelief is also the conscious rejection of a specifically Christian way of looking at the world. But to engage in such a rejection is to enter an unknown world. The Christian faith has played an important part in shaping the world that we know. The core beliefs of Christianity have helped to shape many of the values that the West has taken as axiomatic in understanding what it means to be human. To reject the basis for those values is either to reject the values themselves or to seek a new foundation for many of those same ideas.

For much of our century it has been assumed by an emerging secular tradition that an appeal to reason alone will be sufficient to create the basis for a new civilisation – a new world order. But just as a new world order (based on liberal, democratic and capitalist structures) seems to be triumphant, new doubts are emerging. These doubts enable us to look afresh at our beliefs and hopes. Against all expectations, the question of religious belief is back on the agenda.

This new questioning reveals that unbelief is not the same thing as no belief. It is becoming increasingly clear that we all believe something. The question is not whether we believe so much as what we believe and why we believe it. The recognition that we all have beliefs raises the additional question of what it is that shapes the framework of our belief.[1] The intention of this book is to explore the faith, or faiths, which influence our age of unbelief.

Let me declare my own convictions and the experiences which help to shape my own position. I am a Christian minister. I was born in India, the son of Christian missionaries. My early upbringing was in Scotland. In my mid-teens my family moved to England. In case you should be in any doubt, the cultural difference between Scotland and England is a significant matter! My training for the ministry was in multicultural Birmingham. This experience was further enhanced by living and working in the United States while in my mid-twenties. My first (and formative) ministry was in a multicultural church in inner-city Birmingham. There were ten different nations represented in that church. Approximately 40% of the congregation were of Afro-Caribbean origin and 15% were from various countries in Asia.

My second experience of ministry has been suburban Birmingham. Throughout this time I have been privileged to travel to various parts of America, Africa, Asia and Europe. I have delighted in the company of many who have called themselves "unbelievers" but who have made it very clear that they have all kinds of beliefs about religion, the world and themselves. In all of these friendships I have remained convinced about the worth of the Christian faith and have not hesitated to debate with those who hold very different convictions. I have learned a great deal from those who do not agree with me and value their continued friendship.

Apart from any Christian convictions, I am also sure that our culture is undergoing a period of far-reaching change. Of course, in one sense every culture changes and needs to do so in order to remain healthy. But the change that is presently impacting the culture of the Western world is more significant than the normal developments that influence culture. It is a change that is affecting the way that we think about ourselves, the world in which we live and the way that we relate to that same world. In short, it will eventually influence every aspect of our thought and lives. Because we are in the midst of this change it is hard to see the precise shape of that which is impacting us, but most thinking people are aware that some very profound developments are taking place and are beginning to guess at what they might be.

I am also convinced that the church has an important part to play in this new ferment. This conviction might sound very strange indeed. The church has hardly been on the cutting edge of creative change within Western culture in recent years. All too often the church has been cast in the role of resisting change, or at least arguing for changes which seem to look backwards rather than forwards. But this does not have to be so. The message that has been entrusted to the church contains much that can challenge a culture in ferment to look beyond the superficial, to dare to dream about a new world order that will have more foundation than the exercise of naked political aggression.

During my travels over the last few years I have been impressed by the number of thoughtful, gifted and highly committed individuals that I have met who have become Christians in recent times. Many of these people have not come from a Christian family and have often had to overcome considerable opposition from family and friends to make such a step. Some of these people are now in Christian ministry, or they are considering ministry, or they are beginning to exercise leadership at a local level in their church. These many individuals are but one sign of many positive changes that are taking place in the life of the church at this time. There is every indication to believe that the church that is emerging from its long slumber will be a church that can contribute something vital to our changing culture.

So who is this book for? For many reasons, it is more likely to be read by thinking Christians than by those who stand outside of the Christian tradition. Yet I hope it will also be read by many who would not necessarily describe themselves as Christians but who are feeling towards some of the issues raised in these pages. I would like to think that some, if not all, of these issues are matters that interest and affect thoughtful people regardless of their convictions.

In some ways this has been an uncomfortable book to write, so I suspect that at points it may also be an uncomfortable book to read. There is no deliberate intention to disturb, but inevitably the issues that are dealt with are disturbing because of the sensitivity of all matters of faith and belief. A sense of discomfort is also present because of what the 20th century has witnessed. William Rees-

Mogg describes our century as one which has been full of horror, "...a century of hell on earth for billions of people"[2] He suggests that the painting by the Norwegian artist, Edvard Munch, entitled *The Scream*, and painted in 1893, acted as a prophetic warning of what the 20th century was to experience. Rees-Mogg wonders if there are any voices of hope that might provide illumination for the millenium to come.

This is not a book that provides answers to all the questions that are raised in these pages although I hope that it suggests some answers. I hope even more that it provokes some readers to find additional answers. In this sense, *The Faith of the Unbeliever* is intended as a contribution to a debate rather than a provider of solutions.

Martin Robinson
April 1994

CHAPTER ONE

THE DRAMA OF OUR TIME

We had just finished filming a short item to be included in a documentary series on the church in Britain and there was time for a brief conversation with the producer. He explained that normally he filmed current affairs programmes because he found it very difficult to obtain funding for religious programming. I was aware of some research on audience numbers for religious programmes. The audiences were much higher than I had expected them to be and so I was surprised to discover that it was difficult to find funding for programmes that had such good audience ratings. The producer explained that it was not just a matter of ratings. More importantly, those with whom he had to deal simply did not believe that any thinking people took religious faith seriously. Neither they nor anyone they knew had strong convictions about any faith and certainly not about the Christian faith. From their perspective the Christian faith belonged on the margins of society and did not deserve to be treated seriously by mainstream broadcasting.

Such a view contrasts sharply with the vision that motivated the founder of the BBC, John Reith. The conviction that fired Reith was his view that the BBC should be a vehicle for the propagation of Christian faith and values. What seems remarkable now was not that Lord Reith held such views so much as the fact that his convictions were largely held as being self-evidently right by his contemporaries. It was not that everyone shared such views – the historical record demonstrates that they did not,[1] but the dominant view of European society, whatever people's private morality and public attendance at worship might have been, was that Europe was first and foremost a Christian continent. European, and more generally Western, civilisation was seen as a broadly Christian force, embracing Christian values and beliefs, even if few thought very hard about what those values and beliefs might mean. Today, hardly more than fifty years after Lord Reith's stewardship of the BBC ended, such a value system is seen to be totally unthinkable and even a little barbaric.

The idea that Europe is in some important sense a 'post-Christian' continent is widely accepted as an accurate description of the position. It is not that there are no longer any Christians in Europe, or that there are no longer any links between State and church. The church still has some influence. But the Christian faith and its values no longer dominate the public life of our continent. Politics, business, education and the communication industry all operate on the basis that they need pay no attention at all to Christian ideals and teaching.

Admittedly, the situation is sometimes obscured by the occasional insistence that those countries with strong State churches can in some sense be viewed as Christian societies. The majority of the population in Denmark still pay their church tax and have their children baptised in the State church. All children in Denmark, whether their parents are Protestants or atheists, must have their births at least registered by the church. Yet despite these strong connections with the church, only 1.5% of the population attend any church in that land.[2] People seem to feel that the payment of the church tax guarantees the services of the church when they are needed for such matters as weddings and funerals, without anyone actually having to attend. It is almost as if the church is being paid to keep quiet and leave people alone.

The effect of strong State churches has been to disguise the separation between faith and culture that has been taking place. It is as if the church in these situations has baptised the new culture of the West in a way that fails to recognise that the new culture can no longer be identified with the Christian faith. To be baptised in such a manner says more about being a citizen of a particular country than it does about a person's actual beliefs.

So, for example, in Sweden until 1860 '...it was forbidden for a

Swedish citizen to leave the Church of Sweden; Swedish citizenship unquestionably implied membership in the Church.'[3] Today, even though it is now possible to leave the church, very few actually do. About 5% of the population belong to other churches. Yet according to the same study cited above, only 8% of Swedes '...adhere to a Christian world view.' Since those who belong to other churches make a clear choice in so doing, they make up a very high percentage of the 8% who lay claim to clear patterns of Christian belief. The existence therefore of strong State churches tends to obscure the depth of the change that has taken place.

The situation in the United States is rather more complex. Some indeed have talked about America as a 'post-Christian' nation. But such comments are made in the context of the claim of some 80% of Americans to be affiliated to a church. How can we explain such conflicting evidence? Many have observed that what has happened in the United States is a process of the 'civilising of religion' in order that it might serve largely secular and temporal ends. During the early 1950's the status of religion in the United States assumed a position of semi-establishment. In 1952 a National Day of prayer became an annual event. It might seem strange to us now to reflect that the phrase, 'under God' was formally added to the Pledge of Allegiance in that land only in 1954, while as recently as 1956 the official motto of the United States became, 'In God We Trust'.

One African scholar familiar with the situation in the United States commented in the 1970s:

'America has nearly become a kind of God, and the American Way of Life a kind of religion. There is so much piety in Washington, DC that a church leader can get away with a God-is-dead declaration, while a president cannot survive without paying lip service to a generalised American God. The religious sensitivity of the people becomes dull, and religion becomes a handmaiden of the national purpose, and at times serves cheap, even immoral, political ends.'[4]

In the sense that it is only this kind of tame, domesticated faith that passes as Christianity in America, that land can be properly described in an important sense as 'post-Christian'. As in Europe, public policy is conducted without reference to a biblical agenda, but rather listens to another faith, a civil and secular faith, even if that faith seems to have a strong Christian veneer.

These two changes in the public life of two different countries within the Western world are symbolic of profound changes in the common civilisation of the West that have become evident only during the latter half of the twentieth century. What we have witnessed is the gradual divorce between Western culture and the Christian faith. As Pope Paul VI noted as long ago as 1975, this separation is 'without doubt, the drama of our time'. [5] For us as participants in the drama, the significance of what has taken place is hard to grasp. It is often left to those outside of Western culture to critique and to wonder at the vast changes which, taken together, have produced this great divorce.

The immensity of this change appears all the more dramatic when we remember the part that Christianity has played in shaping and indeed creating the very Western culture which has now declared its independence from that faith. There can hardly be any doubt that the two most important formative influences on Western civilisation have been the classical Graeco-Roman inheritance combined with the Judaeo-Christian contribution of the Bible and its teaching.

These two pillars of Western culture came to our modern world, not as separate streams of thought, but as one integrated whole fused by a single spirituality. As Henry Chadwick points out,[6] it was above all else the world-renouncing monks of the dark ages who helped to preserve education, learning and the inheritance of Greece and Rome, so that they could be transmitted to the emerging medieval world. This fusion of faith and culture in the laboratory of the monastery did much to lay the foundations for the common Western culture that flows to us today. But it is precisely this fusion between Christianity and culture that has dramatically unravelled during the 20th century. The rise of an all-sufficient modernity has presented such a profound challenge to the spirituality represented by Christianity, that the Christian faith no longer acts as the guiding beacon for our culture.

Conflict and a crisis of culture

The gradual separation and divorce that has developed between Western culture and the Christian faith cannot be characterised as a 'clean break' divorce. Both parties live in connected worlds and this inevitably has painful consequences for both partners. As we shall see in the next chapter, the divorce settlement proposed by the forces of modernisation was that those with religious convictions should restrict their thoughts to the private world of opinions, leaving the forces of modernity free to determine the course of public affairs. To a very large extent this is the settlement that has prevailed. Even when Christians have protested against it, they have been largely powerless to change this pattern in the public life of the West.

But the imposition of this settlement by the more powerful partner has not always allowed a happy outcome, even for the dominant forces of modernity. Some very large and inconvenient chickens are coming home to roost. Some of these relate to the profound crisis in our culture that some have described as a crisis of authority. Such a crisis goes deeper than simply the reporting of social problems. We are all aware that drug abuse, together with the crime that accompanies such a trade, is devastating the life of many inner cities in the Western world. We know about the creation of an underclass in society which looks all too like the worst spectres of Orwell's *1984*. The rise in crime, the increase in violence, the return of fascism to the European stage, the increase in nationalism and the settling of ancient scores, these and many other problems are familiar enough to us all. But although these problems might be cited as symptoms of a deeper problem, the mere cataloguing of such social ills can still be dismissed as belonging to the margins of society. These issues are inconvenient, we might wish that they were not there, but life still goes on regardless.

However, the real crisis of which we speak does not lie on the edges of our culture (although it can be found there too). More importantly, it lies at the very centre of Western culture. It can be felt by the young, those gifted people in our universities, who in more stable times, would be preparing to lead tomorrow's world with a sense of certainty and vision. It is abundantly clear that a vision of a hopeful future is not significantly present on the university campuses of the West today. That is not a problem that belongs only to the next generation. It is above all the problem of our whole culture. The West has removed the moral and cultural foundations of an earlier Judaeo-Christian tradition and it has not found an adequate replacement. Commenting on the tumultuous year of 1989 in Europe as walls literally came tumbling down, Os Guinness describes this crisis as it affects the United States:

> But if 1989 marks the start of a momentous new chapter in what was once the Old World but is now the new, it also throws light on a critical state of affairs within the nation that was always modernity's 'first new nation' and the epitome of liberal democracy – the United States. The reason for this sober examination is that, despite its historic political and economic triumphs, the American republic is entering its own time of reckoning, an hour of truth that will not be delayed. It is nearing the climax of a generation-long cultural revolution, or crisis of cultural authority. Under the impact of modernity, the beliefs, ideals, and traditions that have been central to Americans and to American democracy – whether religious, such as Jewish and Christian beliefs, or civic, such as Americanism – are losing their compelling cultural power.[7]

It is not that Western civilisation is about to collapse despite the very serious strains that are evident within it. The problem is perhaps best summed up by the Chinese theologian, Carver Yu, in his succinct description of Western culture as containing 'technological optimism and literary despair'. Technology continues to press the frontiers of knowledge with ever more startling discoveries, nowhere more so than in fields such as genetics and physics, while the fields of art, literature and ethics convey a sense of hopelessness that lies at the root of our culture. One essay produced by a government think tank carries the subtitle, 'Successful economies are no proof against crime, family collapse, and disorder.'[8] The technology of the West is dazzling but it provides no help in healing the core relationships in our society. Indeed we can even argue that it has often acted to exacerbate the strains that already exist.

Faced with signs of social stress, in particular a rising crime rate, politicians have a tendency to begin talking about morality and, in such a context, the role of the churches. Having consigned the role of faith to the margins of society, the church is called upon to somehow 'make people good'[9] without much explanation as to how the church is supposed to accomplish such a task. There is a longing for a return to more certain times. The memory of an older Christian morality which used to be supported by active Christian faith is recalled under the title 'traditional' or sometimes 'family' values. Such an appeal has little intellectual foundation once it has been stripped of its explicit Christian content. Instead of making a consistent moral case, there is a tendency for politicians to argue for what their constituents find acceptable, rather than what is fundamentally right or wrong in itself.

There seems to be no centre to our culture besides a dominant and successful materialism. Does this matter? Certainly there are those who think that it does. The historian Kenneth Clark, commenting on this critical change in the culture of the West notes, '...there is still no centre. The moral and intellectual failure of Marxism has left us with no alternative to heroic materialism, and that isn't enough.'[10] It is this sense that somehow our culture is incomplete, or seriously inadequate in some ill-defined way, that contributes to a feeling of crisis. But how did the challenge to Christianity, which has resulted in the removal of the Christian faith from the centre of Western culture, take place? Given that Christianity both lived with and benefited from the insights of modernity for a full two hundred years before any seriously damaging conflict with the forces of modernity became evident, why should such a divorce take place at all?

The origins of estrangement

The attack of popular atheism

Despite the fact that very few people in the West are what we might call ideological atheists, a good many more are practical atheists. Within that stream of practical atheism has come a very determined attack on the Christian faith. The heart of that attack has been to use the insights of modernity against Christianity. It suggests that Christianity and Science, Christianity and freedom (as expressed in democracy), Christianity and the forces of the Enlightenment, and even Christianity and social progress are implacable foes. The Christian faith in general and the church in particular are seen as standing against these desirable developments in Western (and increasingly global) culture. The suggestion is therefore that all would be well with Western culture (and so the world) if the reactionary past represented by Christianity could somehow be eliminated.

The aim of such critics of Christianity is the creation of a modernity without religion. One Christian industrialist has commented on the fact that many of his good friends work hard to eradicate all religious values in public life on the basis that religion is intrinsically evil.[11] Os Guinness quotes the president of American Atheists as declaring, 'American Atheists is forever opposed to religion and we remain convinced that this world would be the best of all possible worlds if 'faith' was eradicated from the face of the earth'. Guinness implies on the same page that this view represents a kind of secular fundamentalism, as vicious in its own way as the fanaticism of those who follow the Iranian ayatollah's.[12] The late lamented musician John Lennon gives expression to this 'secular fundamentalism' in his song 'Imagine'. Paul Edwards, the editor of *The Encyclopaedia of Unbelief* proclaims that '...the decline of religion will be of incalculable benefit to the human race.' He describes religious principles as 'sick dreams' and suggests, 'The sooner these sick dreams are eliminated from the human scene, the better.'[13]

Matters are rarely so simple! Precisely because the Christian faith and the development of Western culture have been so inextricably connected, it is at best a very simplistic analysis for those who want to criticise Christianity to claim that all the evils of our modern world are caused by religion in general, and Christianity in particular, while all that is good in our culture comes from elsewhere. Those who wish to make such claims have to conveniently overlook the fact that most of the pioneers of the modernity that they espouse were convinced Christians.

Objectors to such radical criticism have good grounds for insisting that the Christian faith has made an important and positive contribution to the development of modernity. They could point to the role of the Christian faith in promoting the progress of the individual, in resisting totalitarianism in all its forms, in pioneering education, health care, social welfare, modern democracy, the rights of the working classes and even, paradoxically, the beneficial wealth creation contained in capitalism.

But despite the rather exaggerated evangelical fervour of these opponents of Christianity, it would be just as foolish for Christians to claim that the church has a monopoly on all things good. Those of us who live in Europe are only too aware that our Christian inheritance has been a two-edged sword. On the one hand it has helped to produce a common civilisation with startling achievements in the arts and the sciences, as well as in specifically religious matters. (The recent talk amongst politicians of both Eastern and Western Europe of a common European home is to some extent a longing to return to the stability and creative order of an earlier Christendom. In that time, a common language [Latin], a common social system, a common religion and a common world view held together diverse peoples in a remarkably stable, single civilisation.) But, on the other hand, we also live with an inheritance in which the Christendom of the past was painfully fractured by religious wars. Europe is the continent both of Leonardo da Vinci and of the Inquisition. Such pain is part of the common folk memory of Europe.[14] In short, the attack of popular atheism has a point but it also contains many flaws.

The spread of secularism

The attacks of popular atheism depend to a very large extent on the broader background of secularism. It is important to note that there is a profound difference between secularisation and secularism. Secularisation describes the process by which societies separate themselves from the control of religious authority in general. For the most part, the process of secularisation by itself does not need to imply a threat to religion and can even be welcomed by Christians as something that is potentially positive. Theologians such as

Dietrich Bonhoeffer with his concept of 'religionless Christianity' and others such as Paul Tillich, and to a lesser extent John Robinson, attempted to embrace this positive dimension of secularisation with a celebration of the secular world. Not that they did so without some awareness of the dangers of such an approach. Tillich in particular clearly saw the limits of emphasising the secular to the exclusion of all religious language and expression.[15] But secularism as compared to secularisation is rather different. Secularism as an ideology carries with it the express intention of eradicating a religious explanation of the world in which we live. It is not so much a specific attack on Christianity in the rather crude manner of the practical atheists, as it is an attack on every religious faith. The theologian Dan Beeby writes of secularism:

> Secularism is when the creature declares the Creator redundant. So the challenge we are to consider is not from the truly secular but from the secular standing in the holy place – an 'abomination of desolation'.[16]

For Beeby, the challenge of secularism is not just to Christianity, but to any notion of truth, freedom and dogma in the sense of declared faith. Together with Newbigin and others, Beeby sees the true nature of secularism, not as opposing faith but as constituting another faith. He asks:

> Is secularism really secular, or is it merely a new form of humanity's oldest ailment – the worship of a humanly-created god? Is the challenge not a secular challenge after all but the challenge of another religion? Are the knowledge and the power and the wisdom of secularism also faith-based? [17]

As we will argue in more detail in the next chapter, the real nature of secularism as another faith has largely remained hidden as Christianity has attempted to come to terms with the forces of this modern age. The State churches of Europe, just as much as the *civil* church of America, have accommodated secular thought to such an extent that the dominant problem of the Church in the West has become that of nominalism – that situation where many are Christians in name only.

I was struck by the story of one pastor in Denmark who told me that one of his church members was elected to the Board of a nearby parish church. This person was a devout believer, but soon became aware that such a qualification was not necessary to be a member of the church board. Some of the board members were the nominees of one of the political parties. The person in question asked if the meetings could begin with prayer but was refused. She continued to ask at every meeting for prayer to take place until at last the Chairman took her aside and advised her to separate her personal faith from her position on the church board.

By contrast, public prayers are regularly offered in the secular parliament buildings in Britain. This practise is an inheritance from the time when the ethos of parliament was self-consciously Christian. Although there are members of parliament in Britain who are Christians, the working assumptions of parliament are no longer governed by Christian doctrine. One has to ask whether the effect of public prayers in a secular parliament are actually much different from the refusal to have prayers on a secular church board in Denmark?

A secularised church produces nominal faith and a nominal faith does not contain the power to resist the advance of other faith commitments. Still less can it become a missionary or converting force itself. It is precisely the question of the conflict of faith commitments and not, as used to be thought, the conflict between faith and the absence of faith that is at issue in the West today.

The secularisation thesis

Although it is certainly true that some elements of secularisation theory have their origins in secularism, the theory of secularisation is not identical to secularism. Indeed some of those who have advanced this theory have been Christians who have not necessarily liked what they have claimed to observe. There are a number of forms of the secularisation theory, but at its most basic the thesis argues that the advances associated with science and with modernisation, (understood as industrialisation and post-industrialisation), continue to erode the social significance of religion.[18] The consequence, therefore, is that public expressions of religion such as church attendance are inevitably eroded with the advance of the modern world. In conjunction with this process a supernatural or magical way of looking at the world diminishes in favour of a view in which mankind sees himself as in control of the world in which he lives.

For many sociologists, it was enough to point to the huge decreases in church attendance seen throughout the continent of Europe during the 20th century to demonstrate the validity of the thesis. Certainly there were exceptions in the Western or modern world to this general European trend, but these could usually be explained with reference to particular local conditions. This has been particularly true of the United States of America, one of the most modern countries in the world, where church membership has remained remarkably constant over the last fifty years. The general expectation of those who adhere to the secularisation thesis is that America has lagged behind Europe in this regard, especially because of immigration, but that eventually it would adopt the same patterns found in Europe. Evidence for this view has been drawn from the observation that those parts of America which seem to be closest to Europe in culture, namely the North East of the United States, seem to exhibit a higher degree of secularisation than those parts which have been further from European culture.

However, over the last twenty years the exceptions to the general thesis have become more and more difficult to explain, precisely because they appear to be becoming more numerous, widespread and diverse. The growing interest in spirituality in the West in general, which has sometimes been labelled as the New Age Movement, but which is wider than such a movement, the growth of those churches in the West which have been rather conservative in doctrine, the arrival and growth of religions from other parts of the world coming to the West as missionary faiths, together with the emergence of religion as an increasingly powerful force on the socio-political world stage, do not yet suggest the kind of inevitable decline of religion that necessarily follows the growth of industrialisation and modernisation.

As you might imagine, the increasing lack of evidence with which to support the secularisation thesis has produced a lively debate amongst sociologists.[19] Some argue that the present upsurge in religious commitment is itself a temporary phenomenon and that soon the inevitable march of secularisation will reassert itself. Others argue that there is no one common explanation for the growth of secularisation and that the various manifestations of increased secularity are both diverse and local.

More interestingly, from the perspective that I have outlined above, a significant number of sociologists have argued that the real difficulty with the secularisation thesis is that it can really only be demonstrated in a European context. This raises the possibility that the process of secularisation has more to do with the culture and belief of some Europeans than it does with the consequences of urbanisation or industrialisation. The sociologist Peter Berger calls such people 'elective Swedes'.[20] By this he means that although one can find movements in other parts of the world which mirror developments in Europe, these have more to do with the history of culture and ideas than they do with modernisation as a single and isolated phenomenon.

The role of the church

The significance of such observations has led some thinkers to look at the complex relationship between Western culture and the church as providing some important clues to the emergence of both secularisation and secularism. The complexity of this interaction is important. New insights into the nature of reality do not emerge in a vacuum. They are partly produced by and depend on that which went before. This is so both positively and negatively. Many scholars have claimed that secularism had its origins partly in the stimulus of the terrible religious wars of Europe, which prompted Europeans to look for other ways of expressing truth.[21]

Still others have pointed to the extent to which the locus of Christianity was important for the development of a secular view of the world which contained a positive view of the possibility of progress, of the essential rationality of man, of the importance of morality as a basis for society and indeed of visions of a future Utopia. (Not a few have described Communism as a Christian sect.) One writer points very clearly to the origin of Western optimism as a crucial ingredient in the formation of secularism. He traces the way in which a biblical world view gives rise to a hope that man can overcome his situation and produce a better future. Moreover, he also notes how this biblical Western tradition has come to the modern world in secular forms. He concludes his analysis by claiming:

> In the West Thomas More immortalised this hope in his book Utopia (1516). However, in Western history the hope is often secularised, as in the French Revolution inspired by Rousseau, in the theory of social evolution, and in the dialectical materialism of Engels and Marx.[22]

In other words, a secular world view was highly dependent on an earlier Christian foundation for the basic optimism contained in its view of reality. But once the accompanying Christian doctrine has been stripped from such a world view, the optimism that is left appears to be shallow indeed. What is its real basis? In attacking the faith which gave it life, secularism has destroyed its own life-blood.

But the dependence of a secular world view on an earlier Christianity has not been easy to detect. It is only as the views of modernity (as represented by secularism) are being forced to defend its core assumptions without the support of a Christian base, that the essential weakness of modernity is becoming clear. The gradual nature of such a revelation relates to the fact that the origins of the estrangement between the Christian faith and Western culture have a long history in the development of the modern, essentially Western world. We are not speaking about a single and decisive break between these two forces. The modern world is not only partly shaped by the past that it wishes to reject, it remains in a complex relationship with that world even as it deals with forces that come to it from a totally different tradition.

The challenge to modernity

In the same way that Christianity gave birth (both positively and negatively) to secularism, the failings of a secular world view have been partly responsible for birthing and shaping the forces which are now challenging its supremacy. Nowhere is this more clear than in the emerging New Age philosophies. The diversity of spirituality contained within a broadly New Age coalition has given rise to some confusion as to whether New Ageism can be described as a single movement at all. Some have detected the presence of an older paganism ranging from a simple pantheism through to the practise of Wicca[23] and even the overtly occult. However, many observers have noted the presence of a variety of Eastern faiths, notably varieties of Hinduism, and have concluded that a large part of the New Age movement is nothing less than the import by the West of Hindu faith and practise.

One astute thinker who has investigated the New Age movement in some depth and who has a sympathetic, if critical relationship with many of its practitioners, has noted that the relationship with Hinduism is a complex matter. In analysing the origins of much New Age thinking, Vishal Mangalwadi points out that there are some significant differences between the Hinduism of the East and the way in which Hindu concepts have been translated in the West by the New Age movement. Not the least of these differences lies in the contrast between the essentially pessimistic world view of the East as compared to the intrinsic optimism of the New Age movement. Mangalwadi comments:

> The New Age accepts the Eastern metaphysical theory that the human self is the divine self. But the deeply ingrained optimism of the Western psyche does not permit it to accept the pessimistic implications of the metaphysics. Therefore the New Age seeks to transform the Eastern view by making it mean that because the human self is the divine self, therefore the infinite self of man should be able to transform his universe.[24]

This strand of optimism is crucial for the formation of New Age thinking. As we have seen, the root of this optimism depends crucially on the impact of the Christian view of hope in the culture of the West. The challenge of New Age ideas to both secular thought and to Christianity therefore depends on the import of.hope from the very systems that it attempts to debunk.

The emergence of an intrinsically religious challenge to modernity has come as something of a surprise to many observers. Religion seems to be back on the agenda. But we should not conclude that Christianity is now able to reclaim its former place in the culture of the West. It is not possible to ignore the all too recent divorce between Christianity and Western culture. Instead, it will be necessary for Christianity to look afresh at its original locus in Western history.

The response of the church

The tension of this separation between Christian faith and Western culture has been a painful experience for the Christian community. There is a growing awareness amongst Christians that the West now represents a mission field. Such a perspective stands in stark contrast to the traditional experience of the church that the West was the secure sending base from which mission was extended to the rest of the world. The connection between Christian mission and the extension of Western influence around the world has been an important feature of the last two hundred years. But that connection is now being broken. For the first time, almost since the first few years of its inception, Christianity is no longer a European religion. It is only since the 1960s that Christianity can truly be called a world faith in the sense that it has a significant indigenous presence in every continent of the world.[25] Since the 1970s the epicentre of Christianity has moved from Europe and North America to the Southern hemisphere. The typical Christian is now an African. In the 1990s it is African States that describe themselves as Christian nations and for whom such a designation really matters.[26]

This shift in the geography and growth of the church is not just a matter of where Christians now happen to live. It forms part of the process of fundamentally altering the self-understanding of the church. The church is now the community of the poor speaking to the rich. It is the two-thirds world speaking to the one-third world. It is above all a people of vision and hope seeking to connect with a culture that has lost hope. John Paul II's encyclical letter *Veritatis Splendor* published in 1993 conveys something of the sense of this new self understanding on the part of the church. The encyclical attempts to outline the broad basis of Catholic teaching on morality. Interestingly, although it was publicised in Western newspapers as a document on birth control, that issue is a fairly minor ingredient in a much broader attempt to look at the moral foundations of society. One cannot escape the sense that the Pope is no longer speaking as the European leader of a Western church, so much as the leader of a church which is increasingly rooted in the two-thirds world and is appealing to the West to listen before it is too late. The feeling that this Christian appeal comes from outside of the West to a Western culture that has separated itself from the Christian faith is surely unprecedented in the history of both the West and the Christian faith.

More recently, Christian writers began to speak of mission as 'Mission to the six continents' (it had previously been only to five continents) and as 'Mission to everywhere and from everywhere'. Christian missionaries from Korea, India, Pakistan, Sri Lanka, Nigeria and Ghana are beginning to appear in the West. But both these new missionaries and the indigenous Christians of the West know that mission in the West is unlike mission in any other part of the world. It is unlike other mission fields because it operates through the filter of a Christian past. That filter fundamentally alters the perception that the Western world has of the Christian faith, and it does so in at least two important ways.

The filter of miscommunication

It is all too easy for those in the West to assume that they already know the content of the Christian message. In fact, it is possible for the West's perception of Christian faith and teaching to be significantly distorted by the communication tools of another faith, namely Western secularism. This distortion leaves people with an astonishingly negative picture of the church in general, even when that negative perception is not matched by personal experience.

A parish church in the London area conducted a detailed survey of their parishioners' views of the church. They received around 200 responses from those who did not attend the church. The survey results demonstrated a warm feeling towards their local parish church, which most respondents had some experience of, but it also conveyed some very negative feelings about the church in general with which they had almost no contact. Why did such prejudicial feelings abound? For the most part the respondents' picture of the wider church had been mediated to them through the press, both tabloid and broadsheet, and by television.

In Britain, the tabloid coverage of the church often seems to extend no further than the idea that it is staffed by naughty vicars who variously run off with their choir mistresses or engage in homosexual acts. While broadsheet coverage is more serious, it tends to focus on such matters as debates about the ordination of women, the shortage of cash produced by the activities of the church commissioners, and the controversial views of supposedly radical theologians or bishops. Furthermore, the closest that many British people come to live contact with a practising Christian is the perception of the church that comes from soap operas. In Britain, such images are the very unflattering ones provided by such productions as *Neighbours* or *Eastenders*. It was precisely these images that were reflected by the survey respondents in London.

It has to be said that the church has all too often lived up to this unflattering image. In the course of ordinary pastoral contact one senses a degree of unspoken anger toward the church, especially amongst older people, which often represents the repressed feelings of earlier hurts, sometimes even of painful childhood memories. The church often does fail. Michael Fanstone's devastating study of why people leave the church contains the damning phrase, '...for many people it was simply a relief to leave the church.'[27] But such failings, real or imagined, do not tell the whole story. The communication gulf caused by no contact at all with a church is probably more significant than the breakdown of communication within a church caused by pastoral failures.

One minister I know spent a good deal of his time talking with young people on the streets near his home. He invited them to come to church. The response was often, 'Oh no, it's too cold.' He was puzzled by this reply. He knew that his own church was well heated so where had this perception come from? He asked more questions and then discovered that during religious education at school they occasionally went on visits to local places of worship to see what they were like. For some reason they had always visited local church buildings which were very large and because it was during the week the heating was not switched on. These children had often frozen while the various aspects of the church building were explained. The miscommunication caused by this kind of rather tenuous contact provides a constant filter of misunderstanding as to what the Christian faith really is.

The filter of failure

The filter of the past conveys the impression that Christianity has been tried and found wanting. Nowhere is this more so than in the supposed conflict between science and religion. It is of course true that there has been conflict between Christianity and Scientism. This is not the same thing as conflict between science and Christianity. Indeed the founders of the Royal Society for Science in the 1660s were committed Christians who were convinced that by understanding the way in which God had created the world, they could only strengthen faith. Many Christian scientists have stood in this tradition ever since. However there is a conflict between Christianity and Scientism, or what Mary Midgely has called 'Science as Salvation'.[28] This all-important distinction between science and Scientism has not percolated to the mind of the wider public. The consequence of this misunderstanding is the widespread fallacy that Christianity in general, and the Bible in particular, has been proved by science to be untrue and is therefore not worth considering.

The benefits of a scientific advance are easily demonstrable in technological terms. But the shortcomings of an entirely reductionist view of our world are also becoming very clear. The essential interconnectedness of the eco-systems of our world are beginning to become apparent. An increasingly religious dimension in the debate about our world and our place in it is beginning to emerge. However, Christianity has been so damaged in the debate with the Scientism of the past, that it has found it very difficult to re-enter the arena now that the possibility of new understandings have arrived. The writer Mangalwadi describes this process very well:

From the beginning Scientism was an absurd and self-defeating philosophy. But by the beginning of the twentieth century, science had acquired power and Christianity had become weak. Therefore it could not effectively point out that reason could not possibly comprehend a non-rational universe, and that Scientism was an emperor without clothes. As this inherent contradiction within Scientism became apparent, and it could not logically defend its faith in reason, it was left to Hinduism, Buddhism, and Taoism to mount the attack on the absurdity of Scientism. Hinduism could attack Scientism because it never had the kinds of problems which Christianity had with science.[29]

As Mangalwadi goes on to demonstrate, Hinduism never had to tackle science at a time when science was intellectually unchallenged, but neither could it have nurtured or produced a scientific method in the first place. Science is the legitimate child of Christianity, but in rejecting its parent through the conflict between Scientism and Christianity, it appears that the parent no longer has anything to contribute. The filter of that past conflict no longer allows Western man to see the potential contribution of the Christian faith.

These two factors, the filter of misinformation and the filter of apparent failure leave the church in the West in some distress. Interestingly, the church has faced this precise dilemma before in one other area in its history, namely the encounter with Islam. Missionaries in Islamic countries know only too well that there is a veil of misunderstanding amongst Muslims about Christianity. Many Muslims have a very distorted view of Christian teaching. A common misconception is that Christians worship three Gods – God the Father, God the Son, and Mary the mother of Jesus. In addition to this veil, Muslims strongly believe that Islam has superseded Christianity, in short that Christianity has been tried and found wanting and that Islam represents something better – an improvement on what went before. The heartland of traditional Islam in North Africa, the Middle East and Turkey are all areas that had significant Christian populations before the rise of Islam. The idea that something has been superseded is a difficult notion to overcome.

The presence of these powerful filters means that the Christian church needs to engage in three tasks.

First it is important to understand something of the history of ideas which has given rise to the present tensions between Christianity and Western culture.

Secondly, there is a need to understand something of the content of the beliefs that men and women in the West now hold.

Thirdly, the church must consider creative ways of engaging with the peoples of the West in order to communicate the message which gives the church its life and meaning.

The various sections that follow in this book attempt to begin such a task under these three broad agendas.

CHAPTER TWO

ORPHANS IN THE UNIVERSE

The way in which we view our world is influenced by what we believe to be the truth about the world. In much the same way, our world view influences what we are able to believe. It acts as an important filter for all that we see and experience. The development of ideas that began with a clear view of the Fatherhood of God and ended by concluding that we are in fact orphans in the universe forms the background to the process of secularisation which was discussed in the previous chapter. But how could ideas change so dramatically? The arrival of the modern world depended critically on the insights provided by the 18th century movement that we now call the Enlightenment.

Given that most of the founders of the Enlightenment were convinced Christians, why should this movement turn out to be so hostile to Christianity? Some have suggested that the 18th century Enlightenment did not come of age until 1968! By this they mean that the turbulent years of the student rebellions in France and across the Western world finally revealed the extent to which Enlightenment ideas, begun on a Christian foundation, had taken a significantly different direction in their later development. This later direction, so hostile to Christianity, in turn produced its own modern myths and its own powerful apologetic. The great strength of modernity lies in the obvious ability of science and technology to provide material benefit to those who embrace its methods. It is essential to understand the background of ideas which led to this profound change in Western culture if we are to understand modernity itself.

32

What's in a world-view?

The medieval marriage of Christianity and Western culture in existence before the arrival of the Enlightenment not only produced a single culture which we know today as Christendom, it was made possible because that cultural framework was underpinned by a single world-view. The collapse of that single medieval world-view introduced a significant fracture in the seamless robe which had been the accepted world of knowledge and faith throughout medieval Europe. In the medieval world, to be an atheist was to be an outcast, not because of the oppression of society, but simply because such a view was unsustainable in the light of what ordinary people took to be self-evidently true. The framework of ideas which people consider to be self-evidently true is intimately related to what we call a world-view.

What do we mean by the term 'world-view'? Lesslie Newbigin offers the highly usable definition that a world-view is what we think about the world when we are not really thinking. In other words, it is that in-built set of assumptions that we make about reality which for most practical purposes we just do not question.

The anthropologist David Burnett describes the notion of world-view as having three critical features. He notes that:

1. A world-view is different from culture but it gives significant shape to the assumptions that a culture makes.
2. The ideas and values of a particular world-view seem to be self-evidently true to those who share that world-view.
3. Our world-view is the means by which we bring order and sense to the experiences and information that come to us day by day. In short it acts both as a filter and as an organising principle.[1]

Because they are so all-embracing, world-views do not change very easily. They tend to be rather stable systems which only alter when it can be conclusively demonstrated over a significant period of time that they do not offer an explanation of reality that fits the information that is available to a particular culture. The work of Galileo, Copernicus and others acted as catalysts in the late medieval period to produce a period of radical questioning and doubt which ultimately caused the collapse of the dominant world - view of their own time. What was so special about the insights offered by these two men? It has been argued that the discoveries that the world was round and not flat, and that the earth was only one planet which moved around the sun, rather than the sun around the earth, were sufficiently revolutionary as ideas that this information caused many other areas of knowledge to be re-examined. So great was this re-examination that it was eventually not possible to simply adjust the earlier medieval world-view to take account of new insights. It had to be abandoned altogether.

Although it is certainly true that since the collapse of a medieval world-view there has never been one world-view to which everyone in society could subscribe, there has nevertheless emerged one particular world-view in the West which has been so dominant that every other world-view has had to take account of it to some degree. That world-view has been so pervasive that until recently, (interestingly only since its assumptions have been questioned), it has not been possible even to name it. It has simply been identified as the way people in the West look at the world. Today, it is more commonly recognised as an Enlightenment world-view.

Dominant world-views are tremendously important in forming what some writers have referred to as 'plausibility structures'.[2] In other words, they help to form a framework of thinking which allows a particular society to agree on what is considered to be 'reasonable'. These structures are used by a society to assess ideas which, although they cannot be proven, seem to be acceptable within the bounds of knowledge that are common currency within the dominant world-view.

We can illustrate such a process using the following story. It is a story told by a missionary reflecting on his experiences in Africa.[3] A number of visitors from the West were being shown around a Christian institution of learning. Their guide knew that the visitors' world-view was formed very strongly by an Enlightenment world-view. With a little mischief in his voice, he introduced a respected African elder who was also a practising Christian. 'Tell me Francis,' said the guide, 'Do witchdoctors exist?' The African elder gave a very careful reply. 'We are told they do not,' he said slowly and deliberately.

Here was a clash of world-views taking place between a number of people who shared a particular expression of the Christian faith. The African elder in question had met enough people from the West to know that it was pointless to discuss the existence or otherwise of witchdoctors, or indeed to have a serious discussion of anything related to the spirit world. He knew that for these Western visitors, the spirit world simply did not exist except as an anthropological oddity. Thus, his belief in the spirit world was at best an interesting psychological phenomenon, but it had nothing to do with an actual description of reality.

The illustration that I have just used is likely to be fairly harmless in the sense that we can all smile at it without too many people being offended. Interestingly we can do so precisely because we now live in a time when enough questions have been asked of a mechanistic world-view that those of us who live in the West might now be inclined to take the issue of primal world-views a little more seriously that we once did. But there are other illustrations which could be used concerning the assumptions of world-view which might produce emotions a little closer to rage. Why should this be so? As we have noted above, although they are different, there is an intimate connection between world-view and the assumptions that a given culture makes. These assumptions contain whole sets of unstated values which are regarded as self-evidently reasonable. Any position which seems to challenge these apparently self-evident values is likely to produce significant levels of hostility. Let me give an illustration.

An acquaintance of mine was about to go abroad as a missionary, and as part of his training lived for a time in a college which had a religious foundation but where the students subscribed to a wide range of religious commitments, as well as to no particular religious faith. Perhaps not surprisingly, my missionary friend received very varied responses to the news that he was preparing for mission service. He discovered that it was not uncommon for some to be appalled at the idea that a person would be prepared to go to another people, to another culture and attempt to 'convert' such people to the religious faith of the missionary. They took the view that missionaries who attempted such a task were displaying appalling arrogance. Yet it was very difficult for those who were making such rapid fire judgements to accept that their very judgement, that such a missionary encounter was 'wrong', might itself be part of a very blatant and arrogant form of missionary enterprise. Those who were making such moral judgements would have been horrified if anyone had attempted to prevent them from speaking, even though there was little attempt on their part to listen to or understand the point of view of the missionary that they were attacking. The set of assumptions which lie behind the notion that attempting to convert others is wrong, is in fact derived from a world-view which flows from the Enlightenment and, as many writers have commented, is as missionary a faith as any the world has ever seen.

Such stories of the arrogance of values derived from the Enlightenment are legion. It would be very easy to fill large parts of this book with them. The telling of such tales almost always raises the temperature of the debate somewhat. But what matters is not the stories themselves, almost all of which have their own rights and wrongs contained within them, so much as attempting to understand the nature of the world-view which lies behind such encounters with the Enlightenment.

The world-view of the Enlightenment

A detailed account of how the Enlightenment came into being would need to look at its origins in the thought of ancient Greece, many of whose ideas came to the West initially through the Christian church in the form of Platonism, and then later through Arab influence on Western Christian scholars in the form of the Aristotelian framework of Aquinas. However, the two most obvious and important contributions to the Enlightenment period, or Age of Reason as it is sometimes called, rests with the traditions known as empiricism and rationalism. Both streams of intellectual thought claimed to deal with the central question for any culture, 'How can we know and understand the world in which we live?'

The principle of radical doubt espoused by Rene Descartes almost certainly represents the first critical step in constructing the framework of thought represented by the Enlightenment. Whereas for Thomas Aquinas faith was the means by which knowledge comes, Descartes, perhaps challenged by the changes pressing in on the world of his day, felt the need to construct a system of thought which would only accept as real knowledge those truths that had survived a process of radical doubting.[4] Many thinkers have demonstrated the self-destructive element in Descartes' thought. Ultimately it cannot survive as a system because radical doubt has also to doubt the process of doubt itself. Nevertheless, Descartes' contribution was so important that it became known as the Cartesian revolution.

The advent of the empirical method of the new science pioneered by men such as Francis Bacon and Isaac Newton, introduced the notion that the empirical method of using observation to present a hypothesis for testing and then constructing sufficient tests until the hypothesis had either been proved or disproved, offered a way of arriving at certain knowledge. Once the work of Newton had been accepted, a medieval world view, one which argued that the world could only be understood in terms of the purpose which lay behind it, was effectively ended. In its place came a system of thought which argued in terms of cause and effect. Every effect has to have a cause. To discover that cause by means of an empirical methodology is therefore to explain that which has been caused. The critical question therefore becomes, not why something has happened but how it has happened. So powerful has this framework of ideas become that even when a scientist asks in a technical linguistic sense 'why has something happened?', they are actually referring to the question, 'what has caused it to happen?' The question 'why has it happened?' in the sense of 'for what moral purpose has it happened?' is no longer asked. It is simply a non-question in the context of a scientific world view.

Lesslie Newbigin comments on the impact of the empirical world view: 'Nature – the sum total of what exists – is the really real. And the scientist is the priest who can unlock for us the secrets of Nature and give us the practical mastery of its workings.'[5]

The work of the empirical tradition in science, a development which began largely in Great Britain, was augmented in the field of philosophy by a large number of continental scholars, particularly

in Germany. The most important development by far was introduced through the work of Immanuel Kant, who himself built on the
earlier work of the British philosophers, Bacon, Locke and Hume.
The critical ingredient introduced by Kant lay in his separation of
the world into the knowable world of the senses which could be
observed and understood by science, and the unknowable realm of
religion and ethics. Put very simply, he suggested a distinction
between the world of 'facts' which could be publicly known and
tested and the world of 'opinions' which, however important, could
only ever be matters of private concern.

The social and political context for Kant's thought was the
emergence of the modern nation state. There had been nation states
in the medieval period, but the modern nation state was very
different in a number of important respects. The opening up of the
Americas, the development of trade with the East by means of the
sea route around Africa (which allowed the West to bypass the
Islamic world), and the growing impact of the scientific revolution,
first on agriculture and then on industry, all contributed to a
concentration of power in the various emerging nation states of
Europe that had not been known during the medieval period. This
new technology allowed nation states with relatively small
populations, such as Portugal and Holland, to have an engagement
with the world far beyond the boundaries explored even by
Alexander the Great and the later warrior kings of the Mongols.

Within these nation states, new social groups were assuming
power. Collectively, the emerging middle classes were more
powerful than the monarchs of medieval times. The thinking of the
Enlightenment helped to define the boundaries of power within
these changed economic, social and political arrangements. A
number of basic principles of Enlightenment thinking were
beginning to emerge, most of which (if not all) were important in
empowering the emerging middle classes. The most important of
these principles were:

1. *The embracing of nature.*   Nature was seen as something that
worked according to a set of fixed and essentially discoverable
laws. Nature was essentially understandable and science was the

means by which it could be both understood and domesticated for the purposes and enjoyment of mankind. No longer would Nature be seen as a mysterious or even malevolent entity before which mankind was helpless and insignificant.

2. *The place of the individual.*   The individual assumed a new position of importance. The new place of mankind in the whole world implied a new autonomy for every individual. Each individual had inherent rights apart from their position in society. The rights of individuals helped to define the power and role of government in the new nation states, as well as helping to limit the power of the older monarchies.

3. *The redefinition of the place of belief.*   Issues of religious belief were designated as matters of private belief. In part, as Pannenberg has argued, this development was a reaction to the years of religious war and tension in Europe. But, as suggested earlier, it also flowed very directly from Kant's framework for the theory of knowledge. For Kant there was no implied conclusion that confining religion to the realm of the private reduced the significance of religion in any way. Indeed his view was that this solution safeguarded the self-evident truths of religion from hostile criticism. But he was not able to predict the ways in which his philosophical system would be interpreted and developed.

A change of direction

At this stage in its development the Enlightenment did not suggest any hostile stance towards religion in general or towards Christianity in particular. Indeed all of the thinkers mentioned so far were devout Christians who believed that their work could only strengthen Christian understanding and faith. If the process by which the world worked could be understood, the Creator could be glorified all the more. The biblical mandate to be good stewards of creation could be more faithfully pursued, given the more effective tools which would flow from a fuller knowledge of the creation. Building faith on that which has been demonstrated to survive the rigours of doubt could only place faith in an exulted position. That same faith could have no more exulted position than one which placed it above all critical enquiry as something which was self-evidently true.

But the Enlightenment process did not end there. The ideas pioneered by thinkers such as Descartes developed in a radically new direction in the fertile soil of eighteenth-century France. The interaction between the anticlericalism incipient in French intellectual life, which found very free expression as a result of the forces released by the French Revolution, produced a cocktail of deism, pantheism, atheism and even a reversion to an earlier paganism.[6] This new situation identified Christianity with the forces of an older order now overthrown in the Revolution. To some extent the church obliged those who wished to represent Christianity in this way by identifying itself with the forces that opposed the Revolution.

But despite the fact that philosophies hostile to Christianity had arisen in France, it was not the case that Europe as a whole had adopted a world-view which rejected Christianity as at best unnecessary and at worst untrue and even evil. At least during the early part of the nineteenth century, Christianity and the forces of the Enlightenment lived in easy harmony. But during the nineteenth century, there arose a number of other key thinkers whose work would finally take the Enlightenment in a direction which allowed the very term 'modern' to mean the creation of a world-view, the underlying assumptions of which meant that any view of reality which saw faith as defining, shaping and illuminating our understanding of the world in which we live, was placed very much on the defensive. None of these by themselves were decisive, and indeed all of them were inevitably dependent to some extent on the work of others. But, taken together, the cumulative impact of these individuals was formidable in the development of Enlightenment concepts. Who were these thinkers?

The social analysis of Karl Marx.   The work of Karl Marx with his dialectical materialism, which built upon the earlier work of Hegel, introduced an apparently 'scientific' analysis of man and society. In this framework religious belief was understood to be a reaction which would fade away in the enlightenment produced by a socialist society. Even though we can now see the considerable flaws in the work of Marx, nevertheless his critique of religion has had a devastating effect on the thinking of the twentieth century.

The philosophy of Friedrich Nietzsche. It is now clear that when Nietzsche issued his proclamation in the nineteenth century that 'God is Dead' he meant specifically the Christian God. The actual implications of the work of Nietzsche are perhaps only becoming fully understood in our own century. More will be said about Nietzsche in the next chapter. For the moment it is important to note that his work hugely influenced the fields of both politics and philosophy by placing man at the centre of the universe. For Nietzsche, God was only the creation of man.

The psychology of Freud. The thinking of Nietzsche was given added force by the work of Freud in the field of psychology. Freud offered a way of thinking about God as a projection that operated within the psyche of man and not as an external reality. Despite the work of Jung, who understood more of the religious, though not necessarily Christian, dimension of Nietzsche, the foundations laid by Freud have almost produced a perennial conflict between the world of psychology and that of the Christian faith.[7]

The biology of Darwin. The contribution of Darwin, though less obviously connected to philosophy, was in fact critical in that it provided not just a way of explaining biological processes, but a comprehensive story of creation which offered a secular alternative to the explanations previously offered by religion. There can be few biologists whose work has had as major an impact on ethics, sociology and even to a degree on politics. Yet Darwin's story of the origin of species, which strongly implied an 'explanation of everything' in terms of the origins and development of life within the universe, has acted in just such a way. The sense of the moral rightness that the fittest will survive, not just through chance, but because there is an implied rightness about their survival, has permeated the thinking of disciplines in the West far beyond those of biology itself.

How did these applications of the work of Darwin take place? Mary Midgley is surely right to point to the work of secular humanists such as T.H. Huxley who wished to see science as an alternative faith. She comments that many nineteenth century scientists saw science as:

> '...a whole myth, a philosophical conception of the world and the forces within it, directly related to the meaning of human life. They saw this penumbra as part of science because it was needed if scientific proposi- tions were to have their full bearing on the rest of thought.... People like T. H. Huxley meant by science a vast interpretative scheme which could shape the spiritual life, a faith by which people might live. This faith was a competitor with existing religious faiths, not a way of having no faith at all.' [8]

It is the understanding of science as a competitor, another faith, that has helped to create the sense that religion and science have been in conflict and that science has won the day. In the popular mind, science has disproved religion. Actually such a view of science is more properly called Scientism and should be seen as quite distinct from the exercise of pure science. Nevertheless, from this point on, the emerging secularism of the nineteenth century, the self- understanding of the West that it was now in a 'modern era', and even the term the Enlightenment, became so closely identified that at times they are used interchangeably. The world-view of the modern world is avowedly secular. The forces of modernity are the inheritors of the Enlightenment. Man is alleged to stand at the centre of a universe in which he is autonomous. He is an orphan in the universe, but an orphan so powerful that he can be supremely optimistic about his standing and status in the world. The processes by which the universe works are in principle understand- able and, to quote Stephen Hawking, once we do understand them all, 'we will know the mind of God',[9] not because we will have found God but because man will believe he finally stands in the place of God.

The myths of modernity

The elevation of a secular world-view with science at its centre suggests that certain essentially unproven but extremely important convictions underlie or are a consequence of that same world-view. It is these convictions that help to formulate the 'plausibility structures' within which Western society operates. It is therefore very important to be clear as to what at least some of these confining convictions actually are.

Science as a substitute for religion

We have already referred to the sense in which science has become for many a faith which offers a comprehensive explanation of the world in which we live. As theologians faced such a challenge, God became first a 'God of the gaps', that is to say he was used as a way of explaining the gaps in the knowledge of science. However, as scientific knowledge expanded there came an increasing sense that if God existed at all he was profoundly absent. It was not just that he could not obviously be seen directly, but neither could his involvement with the world be clearly demonstrated. Increasingly theologians were pushed to a view of God which saw him only as a kind of first cause, who having set the whole process in motion, had retired to watch the consequences from a safe distance. A number of writers[10] have commented on the degree to which theologians have accepted the framework offered by science, rather than challenging the faith grounds on which science itself actually operates.

What are the faith grounds on which science operates? Two areas are important here. First, there is the necessity for science to act on the basis of a number of faith commitments. Newbigin refers to these as the convictions that 'the universe is rational and that it is contingent'.[11] The exercise of science would not be possible without these ultimately unprovable certainties. As Newbigin also comments, 'It is therefore not an accident that modern science was born in a culture which has been shaped for many centuries by this belief'.[12] In short, science is indebted to a Christian inheritance for this central conviction.

The second area concerns the value of the knowledge offered by science. Whereas initially the empirical method of science was offered as a means of observing how things work under certain conditions, the pursuit of science has often come to be an end in itself, rather than a means to an end. The very act of acquiring knowledge by scientific method comes to assume an intrinsic value, one might almost say a spiritual value quite distinct from the actual value of the discovery itself.[13] This process seems to imbue the scientist with a standing or status which justifies his description, quoted earlier from Newbigin, as a priest, delivering judgements or truth about our world which have the status of revelation because of the certitude that is implied. Such truth simply cannot be questioned. Midgley notes the tendency in more recent times for science to reduce its claims as to what it can really know in any kind of precise way. But she also notes that the contraction of scientific claims to knowledge have not been accompanied by any decline in the status of science as something 'vast, sacred and mysterious'.[14]

This would not be so bad if it were not the case that during the twentieth century many other disciplines have made strong claims to be treated as if they too were engaged in scientific enquiry. Because of its particular place in the Enlightenment, the study of history has been prominent in making such claims.[15] Even more critically the social sciences have made similar claims. These claims are highlighted by the very use of the term 'sciences' in their self-designation. It is the claims of sociologists, psychologists, political theorists and economists, all of whom say that they are engaged in forms of scientific enquiry, that actually impact the shape of society outside of the disciplines of study themselves, because they are involved in a public debate about the nature of reality from which religion is specifically excluded.

It is not that the general public always take the pronouncements of the individual high priests of such sciences too seriously. Even when the Christian faith was the accepted foundation of society, the word of particular theologians or priests did not have to be accepted. But what is accepted without question is the right of those from these 'scientific disciplines' to make pronouncements in the public arena, however questionable their 'findings' might be.

It is precisely this area of public debate that religion is excluded from. Certainly religion is permitted to speak about matters of morality and ethics, but the subtlety of this permission lies in the assumed and frequently stated position that any statements about such matters only really have force in the realm of an individual's private life. There is an absolute refusal to accept that positions arrived at on the basis of a religious conviction can have any binding impact on anyone other than those who hold to such private faith. Personal faith, it is said, is a matter of private opinion, and as such belongs to the world of the subjective and hence by implication is unprovable and thus unimportant. The churches are urged to teach morality, even to give a moral lead, but by implication, only to those who accept the faith statements on which such teaching is based. One has to come to the conclusion that when the churches are urged to act in this way, what is envisaged is more a mechanism for social control than an invitation to enter a genuine public debate.

Faith as private not public truth

The consequence of the distinction between the world of 'facts' and the world of 'beliefs' has been the consistent devaluation of the place of belief in the public arena. The term 'belief' has gradually become equated with the word 'opinion' and the concept of 'values'.[16] Newbigin helpfully illustrates the impact on our culture of this separation by detailing the telling of two stories in British schools. The one is the story of evolution which is taught as 'fact'. The other is the telling of God's dealings with man through the history of Israel and then of the church, which is taught in terms of values. This second story '...if it is taught at all – is taught as a symbolic way of expressing certain values in which some people, though not all, believe. The first is taught as what we know, the second as what people believe.'[17]

The world of facts then has come to mean objective truth which is knowable and can be accepted by everyone living in a society regardless of their beliefs or values. The world of faith or belief on the other hand is equated with a subjective view of knowledge and so is 'only' someone's opinion. Since there are many different opinions it is considered important to respect everyone's opinion and so anyone can believe what they like as long as they do not seek to impose that view on anyone else. It is especially unacceptable for a person to suggest that their view represents some kind of ultimate truth to which everyone should respond. In such a framework the various religions are all equally valid, no matter what their claims may be. A secular framework allows such a privatisation of religious faith and so creates a kind of religious supermarket with a 'pick-and-mix' ingredient. This leads to the conclusion that what matters is not so much what is actually true, but whether it is true for you. The criterion for the adoption of a particular view or practice becomes 'Does it work for you?'

Such an apparently tolerant outcome actually masks an incredible arrogance. The privatised pluralism of the religious supermarket is not really saying all faiths are equally true, so much as they are all equally untrue and therefore it doesn't really matter which one you choose. Secular society implicitly claims that the only real truth is to be found in a public arena dominated by a particular world-view which is based on a whole series of unchallenged faith statements. Within schools a secularist position which underlies educational thinking makes the implicit claim that a secular syllabus can teach all the religions with an unbiased value free objectivity and are often surprised when it is suggested that this might be just a little arrogant. Actually it is breathtakingly, blindingly arrogant! From its dominance in the public arena, a secular 'faith position' attempts to dictate the way in which the great faiths of the world are taught, despite the widespread protests of those faiths that their respective faiths are being challenged without any opportunity to challenge the beliefs of those who are making such an attack.

The erection of a new public creed

In reality, far from abandoning all creeds, the modern world which claims to deal only with 'facts', embraces a number of key beliefs which for the modern world are part of a public creed. This creed flows directly from ideas championed during the 'Age of Reason' (the Enlightenment). There is perhaps no better illustration of the public declaration of these values as facts than the founding charter of the first modern nation on earth, the American Declaration of Independence. 'These facts we take to be self-evidently true...' What are these so-called 'facts'?

1. The Enlightenment presupposes a particular doctrine of the nature of man. Essentially there is a belief that man is naturally good. Rousseau's 'noble savage' has exercised a tremendous power as a modern myth and was itself part of a prevailing spirit of optimism within the Enlightenment.[18] Admittedly, not all of those who inspired the Declaration of Independence were as optimistic about the nature of man as was Rousseau. [19]

2. The idea of goodness was strongly attached to the idea of progress, both moral and material. The Enlightenment presupposed that the forces of science, education and political reform, would bring an enlightened age when mankind would build a new society. For Christians that society was closely equated with ushering in the Kingdom of God. For secular humanists, progress would inevitably mean the decline of all religious belief. Such a decline would not only be a consequence of the modern world, it would help to usher in that same world, a kind of secular utopia, where religion or superstition would fade away.

3. Just as man and not God was to stand as the central concern of the Enlightenment, so the individual and not society was to take centre stage in the emerging modern world. To the degree that society existed at all, it was only the product of individual choice and not a point of reference from which individuals would chart their course. The emphasis was on the rights of man and no longer on his place and duty within society. The importance of the individual implied that a broadly liberal democracy was the final and best possible political expression of modernity. Such a tradition found its finest hour in the apparent defeat of communism and gave rise to the 'end of history' thesis expounded so widely at the end of the 1980s.[20]

4. The oft-stated purpose of life within an Enlightenment world-view was declared to be the pursuit of happiness. The contrast between this view of the chief end of man and that of the Reformation fathers could hardly be greater. The Reformers declared that the chief end of man was to know God and to glorify

him. The puritans were convinced that only in such an end could man know true happiness. What does the pursuit of happiness mean without any concern for the pursuit of the knowledge of God? It would seem to mean whatever the individual wants it to mean, and therefore an essential prerequisite for such a pursuit is the maintenance of personal freedom. Therefore a large part of the agenda of any liberal democracy can be described as safeguarding the freedom of the individual. The debate about the parameters of personal freedom in relation to the rights of others is a complex matter. Suffice it to say that it has become an article of faith in the West that what someone thinks as a private individual should never be the concern of the rest of society, provided that an individual does not seek to physically harm others on the basis of that belief.

The agents of modernity

It is perhaps above all the trumpeting of the values of democracy and personal freedom virtually as religious values, that has marked the encounter of modern Western democracies with the rest of the world. The history of that encounter has been a remarkable story. The ideas that emanate from the West are sufficiently powerful and subversive that many have noted that the West is now to be found in city life everywhere in the world. Some have begun to speak about the emerging economies of the Far East as 'the New West'. Modernity is no longer a purely Western phenomenon. The very spread of Western ideas around the world marks modernity as a strongly missionary faith, one which contains the idea of the inevitability of such 'progress' within its own missionary creed. In exporting its faith modernity has been able to enlist the help of some very powerful tools.

Modernity and education

The world of education has possibly been the most powerful means of exporting a modern world-view. It is the assumptions of the Enlightenment that underlie the educational system that the West has exported with such success. The motivation for the spread of education has not just been the desire to convey new skills to others. The package also includes the idea that the spread of education will end superstition, (such as belief in spiritism), and lead inevitably to the rise of women's rights, (largely as understood by the West), encourage the advent of democracy and indeed hasten the adoption by others of a significantly Western cultural perspective. It has to be said that this is exactly what has transpired in many cases.

But if it is relatively simple to see the full package of consequences that comes with the export of education, it is not always as easy to understand the way in which education has acted in our own culture to teach much more than 'facts'. The problem is not as noticeable at a primary school level where the subjects that are taught do not impinge so directly on world-view, but there seems to be a noticeable shift in the attitudes of children during the first three to four years of secondary school. It is amongst this critical 11–15 year age group that world-views are explored on a subject-by-subject basis. Interestingly, it has often been the members of Muslim, Sikh and Hindu communities, (all of whom see the benefits of education), who have been more acutely aware of the corrosive effects of Western education on religious faith of any kind.

Research in Scotland undertaken amongst 6,095 pupils aged 11–15 demonstrates very clearly some difficulties in reconciling positive attitudes towards science with positive attitudes towards Christianity.[21] The responses received by the researchers show the prevalence of Scientism amongst schoolchildren in this age group. By Scientism they mean 'the view that scientific methods and scientific theories can attain to absolute truth'. Other research cited by the authors of this Scottish research indicates a widespread view of the basic incompatibility between science and religion. That feeling of incompatibility tends to lead to the loss of interest in religion rather than in science, on the basis that it is a scientific world-view rather than a world-view with any religious dimension that offers a valid description of reality.

But the problem of reconciling Scientism with religious convictions represents only part of the problem found in education. The underlying assumptions which are made in all the disciplines taught in our schools have a strong tendency to be hostile to Christian faith. One university lecturer told me of the anguish felt by many of his students who were Christians, because they were often required to give a Marxist or some other secular view of a particular development, but were prohibited from giving a Christian view of the same topic. Those who are working in the field of psychology have noted how the very disciplines of the subject assume that religious faith is a phenomenon which needs explanation. Psychologists do not assume that an interest in art or in music needs explanation. Nor would they tend to look too kindly on a thesis which began with the thought that the apparent need of psychologists to investigate religion might itself be worthy of some investigation. The foundations/ of Western education in the Enlightenment itself has produced a situation where, as Peter Berger (amongst others) has noted, the more educated you are the less likely you are to have an active interest in religious faith.

The irony of this situation has not escaped observers such as Lesslie Newbigin. He points out that Christians have traditionally exported both modern medical care and education as part of their missionary activity. In doing so, it is Christian missions that have sometimes been the most effective exporters of an Enlightenment world view – a view that is invariably hostile to the very Christian faith that sponsors its spread.

2. Modernity and medical advance

Very few countries in the world are able to make secondary education available to their whole population free of charge. However, the advances of medicine in the modern era have a very direct effect on the lives of millions. From a purely personal perspective, I am aware that had I been born one hundred years earlier, then, at the age of five or at the age of eleven, I would almost certainly have died as a result of illnesses which today are considered to carry a relatively low risk to life.

The discovery of the benefits of immunisation and of antibiotics have saved countless numbers of lives. Diseases such as smallpox and even leprosy are no longer the scourge that they once were. The increase of knowledge in the broader field of healthcare has saved even more lives by encouraging the provision of clean public water and proper systems of sanitation. In those societies which have benefited from such change, it is now the normal expectation that a new born baby will survive both the birth experience itself and live long enough to become an adult. We all too easily forget how recent that expectation is in terms of the normal human experience through the centuries.

Such changes have inevitably impacted the way in which we look at our world. In most traditional societies, medicine is closely connected to religious practise. Traditional healers are also the gatekeepers to the stories, legends and self-understanding of a tribe or larger community of people. In the West the connection between healing and the church has been a long and honourable one. The very term which we use to honour our nursing staff, 'sister', has its origins in the care exercised by religious communities of nuns for the sick and dying.

As recently as the mid-nineteenth century the most significant leaders in any English community would be the more substantial land owners, the doctor and the parson. There was a strong possibility that these figures would also be related by marriage. The clergy of the late twentieth-century Western world are well aware that they no longer occupy such a position, not just because of a change in social standing, but because their function has altered. Whereas in traditional societies the power of healing was attached to religious leaders, now the reverse is true. Many doctors are aware that they have taken on some of the functions of priests, even if they are uncomfortable about so doing. More broadly, and building rather explicitly on developments in medicine, psychiatrists, psychologists and counsellors have taken on the roles of listening to confessions, pain, anxiety, family traumas and other neuroses in a manner which has a much more direct parallel to the role of the priest.

There has been a good deal of debate about the effectiveness of modern counselling and psychology as compared to the efficacy of traditional religious practices. Indeed there are many who are working to bring a greater degree of integration in the insights of both traditions. But the importance of the shift that has taken place is not that the counsellor is any more or less effective than the priest, so much as the transition from priest to psychologist marks a change in world-view, a change that has been dramatically reinforced by the observable benefits of medical advance.

Modernity and technology

Whether it was the still pre-modern arrival of the Spanish Conquistadors clad in metal and riding on animals never before seen in the Americas, or the arrival of Captain Cook with his many masted expeditionary ships in the South Sea islands, the first contact between European traders and explorers with native populations the world over often demonstrated from the first the sense of an overwhelming technological power which the West has possessed throughout the modern period.

More recent times have seen the West dominate the world in more complex and subtle ways than the sole exercise of brute military might. But whatever the method used by the West, technological superiority has been a formidable ingredient in the exercise of Western power and influence. The marriage between the pursuit of wealth, the desire to safeguard national interests in that pursuit, and the innovation of technology, has been noted by many commentators from Machiavelli's time to our own. While it is certainly true that there have been many idealists who have seen the potential of technology to bring happiness to all, the reality has not always matched such hopes. At the very least there is a basic tension between the idealistic use of the power that technology brings and its use to preserve the in-built advantage of the powerful. Os Guinness comments:

> Appalled by events in Vietnam, even a great patriot like Walter Lippmann found a new vocabulary creeping into his writing. 'There is a growing belief that Johnson's America is no longer the historic America, that it is a bastard empire which relies on superior force to achieve its purposes, and is no longer an example of the wisdom and humanity of a free society'...Indeed, the greatest nightmare of the secular future will grow out of its deafness to its own noises, its lack of feeling for its self-inflicted wounds.[22]

Others such as E. F. Schumacher have pointed to the connection between an unbridled technological optimism and a modern world view.[23] But despite the warnings of those who see that if modern man was ever to win what is sometimes seen as a technological battle with nature, that man himself would be the loser[24] The gains of technological progress are mostly seen as confirming the validity of the world-view which has brought modern technology into being. In short, the power of technological development seems to confirm the validity of a world-view in which God is absent. As one Dutch saying puts it 'Artificial fertilisers make atheists'.[25]

Beyond belief

The impact of education, medicine and technology in acting as agents of modernity are not the only such influences that are at work. The media and communications industry, modern commerce and industry, and even the way in which politics are pursued, all serve to reinforce the structures of modernity. It is these structures which help to reinforce ideas about reality and the way we understand it. They help to create our view of what is likely to be true or reasonable. Within such a framework, the ideas presented by Christianity do not seem to be very reasonable. Christian claims seem to fall outside of the plausibility structures that modernity has created. This is not the same thing as saying that Christianity is untrue. It only means that the plausibility structures of the modern world make it very difficult indeed to believe such claims. I have sometimes talked with people who have commented: 'What you have said to me about Christianity makes sense and is probably true, but it just isn't an option for me to believe it in any practising sense.'[26]

Those who do choose to believe that the Christian revelation of God is true can do so either as a matter of private belief, perhaps out of some family or traditional loyalty, possibly because it 'works for them', or they can do so as thoughtful rebels. Such a rebellious stance gives new meaning to the word 'nonconformist'. It used to refer to that part of the Protestant church which was part of the tradition of Dissent, those who for the most part were non-Anglicans. Perhaps today, all Christians in the West are called to be dissenters, whether Anglicans, Pentecostals, Catholics, Orthodox or Free Church, to bear witness to that which seems to be 'beyond belief' for many in our society, but which may just turn out to be true, not just for those who believe it, but for all humanity.

CHAPTER THREE

THE PERPETUAL PRESENT

It is more than a little ironic that in the very moment of its apparent strength in the dominance of the Western political system, modernity should be undergoing a severe challenge in the universities and other seats of learning that are themselves the product of modernity. That challenge extends beyond an educated elite. It is echoed in the crisis of culture that I have already described. But why should it be that modernity should be undergoing a challenge in the moment of its greatest triumph. And if this is true, what if anything is likely to replace this once all-powerful system?

A great deal has been written about post-modernism in all kinds of fields, from art to architecture, and from physics to philosophy. But what does such a term really mean? Is post-modernism merely a temporary reaction to modernity which will see the forces of modernity re-establishing their place in our world? Is post-modernism here to stay, or is it merely paving the way for other movements to take their place in our future? Not too much is certain, except that there is now a deep fissure in the landscape of modernity through which a whole range of movements, ranging from the already mentioned post-modernity through to a renewed neo-paganism, are making their presence felt. These new movements are different from one another and yet are not wholly unrelated to each other. How can we understand this new and changing horizon?

The end of modernity

Brian Appleyard has written extensively in his column in *The Times* newspaper on the problems of a modern scientific world-view. In one such piece he quotes the zoologist Richard Dawkin as responding to the idea of man's loneliness in the universe:

> 'I don't feel depressed about it', the zoologist Richard Dawkin told me, 'but if somebody does, that's their problem. Maybe the logic is deeply pessimistic, the universe is bleak, cold and empty. But so what?'[1]

In fact there is a great deal in that 'so what'. The confidence of Dawkin in crying 'so what' in the face of his own assertion that humankind is orphaned in the universe, represents the voice of considerable privilege. The writer Walter Brueggemann helpfully summarises the critique of those who claim that a modern Enlightenment perspective is the view of those for whom such an understanding has worked extremely well. It is above all a white, male and Western standpoint.[2]

Breuggemann, together with many others, believes that the world of the Enlightenment is certainly now coming to an end. He identifies part of the problem of modernity as lying in the fact that it represents a white, male world of Western colonialism which has had its day. From his perspective the politics of the West has a vested interest in pretending that the system is still intact, that it still works, but that in fact its undisputed authority is now questioned to a fatal extent. The nature of this vested interest is sufficiently strong to ensure that the structure of modernity will not collapse in the near future, but ordinary people can feel that its days are numbered.[3] What does he mean by such dire warnings?

Breuggemann is writing in the 1990s, but other writers commented at least ten years earlier that the confidence exhibited by the West as recently as the end of the 1950s now seems to belong to another era, rather than merely to another decade.[4] Such writers remind us that the period following the Second World War was remarkable for its childlike faith in the capacity of science to bring a virtual Utopia into being for those civilised countries that had uncovered its secrets. The benefits of science would ensure that in the future machines would labour on behalf of mankind. The future would be a time of wealth and of leisure for all. Education would eradicate the superstitions of the past which had brought conflict and hatred. Progress, by which was meant technological progress, would bring equality, freedom and happiness. It might now seem incredible that any culture could believe such things in the shadow of the death camps of the Second World War. The emptiness of such a message is now becoming apparent.

It is, above all, the sense that the modern way of viewing the world is unsatisfactory and is now slipping away that is so reminiscent of that earlier change which marked the end of the medieval world and first ushered in the period of the Enlightenment. Rabbi Jonathan Sacks expressed this feeling in his recent Reith Lectures:

> We are caught between two ages, one passing, the other yet not born, and the conflicting tendencies we witness – deepening secularisation on the one hand, new religious passions on the other – are evidence of the transition.[5]

The sense of not being able to remain in the old certainties and yet having no new path clearly defined ahead, produces profound anxiety for our culture. Walter Breuggemann echoes this anxiety as he states:

> At its deepest levels our culture is one in which the old imagined world is lost, but powerfully cherished, and in which there is bewilderment and fear, because there is no clear way on how to order our shared imagination differently or better.[6]

The inadequacy of the 'old imagined world', however powerfully cherished, coupled with an awareness that the modern age is now passing, leaves us with a post-modern horizon which is puzzlingly unclear. Yet some shape can be detected in the themes of post-modernism. At least three themes emerge.

1. The rejection of history. The dominant philosophical framework for post-modernism seems to be utter nihilism. In abandoning the false certainties of science with its particular historical framework, post-modern man has adopted the view that there is no such thing as meaning, and because there is no meaning there is no such thing as history. All historical frameworks presuppose that there is meaning and so look for patterns and explanations with which to illuminate that meaning in history. Such an historical viewpoint seeks to understand not only the past, but on the basis of such patterns, the future also.

2. *The dominance of the present.*   For post-modern man, the rejection of meaning and history means that there is no past and no future, there is only a perpetual and dominant present. A preoccupation with the present brings a deification of encounter with the present. The experiential is the means by which the present is grasped and understood. So, for example, consumerism demonstrates very well a post-modern response to the products that the modern world has created in order to satisfy the physical needs of humankind. In the contemporary shopping mall the goal is to present shopping as an experience of pleasure, worthwhile for itself, regardless of the utilitarian value of the goods that are purchased.

The store of the late twentieth century is a palace of pleasure. The grand piano, the palm trees and the splendid fountains, all contribute to enhance the pleasure of the shopping experience. The point of the purchase is not related to the usefulness of the commodity that is bought, so much as to the pleasure of the purchasing experience itself. The goods become almost incidental and may even be discarded soon after they are paid for. One observer has noted the similarity of many shopping malls to places of worship, except that in these modern cathedrals the emphasis is not on a world to come, so much as on creating a contemporary fantasy experience in this world.[7]

3. *The obsession with power.*   The assertion of post-modern thought that it is misguided to look for patterns of meaning in the universe is not a simple reaction to the earlier modern certainty that the world was bound to progress towards a future Utopia, fired by

the 'white-hot heat of the technological revolution'.[8] The seeds of the post-modern are fully contained in the framework of modernism.

John Milbank argues very persuasively that the central issue of post-modernism and of scientific modernism is the exercise of power. This obsession with power leads ultimately to the loss of any objective meaning beyond that which serves the demonstration of power itself.[9] The unmasking of the real concern of both modernism and post-modernism demonstrates very clearly that the ultimate end of a commitment to nothing but reason is in fact irrationality. The social critic and thinker Jacques Ellul has written extensively on the impact of technology and on the way in which we think about our world. In one particular passage he notes the appeal of the irrational which paradoxically lies at the centre of an obsession with what technology can produce. It is as if we are so overwhelmed by the power of technology that we are unable to see the meaning of such power. The result is that the giving of meaning to any particular action has to be resisted.[10]

Ellul could easily have been describing the post-modern situation. In fact he was describing the outcome of the modern, secular humanist worldview. Post-modernism is not a reaction to modernity, it is the logical outcome of modernity.

Post-modernism and religious experience

Just as the modern world was born as a consequence of new discoveries in the field of physics accompanied by developments in the world of philosophy, so the origin of the post-modern has a very similar parentage.[11] The fixed world of observable scientific laws propounded by Isaac Newton had led both to a determinism (which held that everything could in principle have a predicted outcome), and a reductionist view of life. (By reductionism we mean the idea that the whole can be understood by reference to its parts.) We have seen how in such a universe there was no room for the idea of God. In the famous words of Laplace to Napoleon, 'I have no need of such a thesis'. But developments in the world of physics, most of which are associated with Einstein, began to shake the older certainties which had previously governed scientific method.

The scientist, Rodney Holder, has helpfully outlined the way in which earlier developments in mathematics foreshadowed the work of Einstein in much the same way that progress in mathematics laid the groundwork for Galileo, Copernicus, Bacon and Newton.[12] Speaking of twentieth-century developments in both maths and physics he says:

> Both subjects have been through dramatic and revolutionary change in the present century, and these changes have deep implications. Not only do they revolutionise our view of the world, including the very nature of reality, but they impact in a fundamental way on epistemology, for they reveal clear and unbreachable limits to the knowledge which can be obtained by the methods of science.[13]

The precise reason as to why the discoveries of Einstein and his contemporaries have had such a revolutionary impact on scientific thinking are sufficiently complex that they cannot be discussed in any detail in this book. Suffice it to say that their importance goes beyond the actual systems themselves. In essence they demonstrated that the mechanistic world posited by scientists since the time of Newton was completely inadequate to take account of the new theories suggested by Einstein in order to explain his findings. Mary Midgley summarises the nature of these difficulties. She writes of:

> ...A split in current attitudes to science. Prudent official modesty, designed to ward off sceptical attacks, clashes with the confidence, the bold vision, which helps people to carry on scientific work. Quantum mechanics is a special focus for this split – a kind of San Andreas Fault – because in it the gap between successful practice and floundering theory is so glaring.[14]

In explaining the dilemma of the post-Einstein phase of science Midgley speaks of the need for science to use poetic language. In this sense, scientists are not so much describing facts as offering images and analogies. Thus the major implication of the startling developments in physics pioneered by Einstein has been to cause many scientists to be more careful in the claims they make about the extent to which science offers an objective understanding of the nature of reality, while at the same time encouraging science to look for more holistic explanations when trying to understand the way in which the world works. This does not mean that there are no longer any reductionists or those who want to make much the same kinds of claims for science that earlier reductionists made. But it does at least mean that such views cannot be propounded without an attempt to justify them as if they were self-evidently true assertions. Although the implications of these new insights have been available within the scientific community for most of our century, the effect of these developments have only begun to percolate other disciplines and the popular imagination in relatively recent years.

The questioning that the new physics has produced has led some scientists to look for a new unity between religion and science. For the most part, many such scientists have looked to Eastern religious traditions to provide a framework for their thought. In part the reason for exploring such Eastern traditions lies with the already-mentioned conclusion that Christianity has both been tried and found wanting, and also because of the extent to which the Christian tradition has been identified, both correctly and falsely, with the tradition of modern science prior to the twentieth century. These attempts are described by Rodney Holder as 'quantum mysticism' and as 'the living earth' or the Gaia hypothesis proposed by James Lovelock. It happens that both these scientific responses to a failed reductionism find their echoes in parallel developments that had been in place for much longer in the field of philosophy.

Although there are important earlier developments in thinkers such as Rousseau, the key figure in the formation of post-modernist thinking is clearly that of Nietzsche. It was he who saw the fundamental flaw in the Cartesian principle of radical doubt which had been such an important foundation for Rationalist thought, namely that in order to be consistent, the principle of radical doubt had itself to be doubted. As Newbigin has expressed it:

The programme of universal doubt, the proposal that every belief should be doubted until it could be validated by evidence and arguments not open to doubt, can in the end only lead – as it had led – to universal scepticism and nihilism, to the world which Nietzsche foresaw and which Allan Bloom and other contemporary writers describe.[15]

It is now recognised that when Nietzsche spoke of man as 'superman' and of God as the creation of man, he was not attacking religion as such. He was certainly not advocating an atheistic position. Rather he was specifically attacking the Christian God and by implication the Christian religion. As Visser 't Hooft comments;

> It is quite wrong to think of Nietzsche as the enemy of religion. It is true that he announces the death of God, but this means the death of the traditional Christian God. Nietzsche really wants to be the founder of the new religion. He has hoped that the new Dionysian era which he described in his 'Geburt der Tragodie' as a 'rebirth of Hellenic antiquity', would be inaugurated through the musical dramatic art of Richard Wagner, but when Wagner proved inconsistent he concocted his own religion.[16]

The nihilism of post-modern thought is not the absence of religious sentiment as a simple cry of despair, nor is it merely a return to religious romanticism conceived as a reaction to religionless liberal secular humanism, or even religionless Christianity. Rather it contains the assertion that science itself is a religion but one which contains a false mythos. The recognition of a false mythos is made in the context of a claim to have discovered true religion, a religion of the senses, one which is experienced and not made known by revelation in history.

The concern of post-modernism is with the natural in all its forms and it is this aspect which has led many observers to call it 'neo-paganism'. However, this is too simple. Although it does indeed contain many aspects of an older paganism, it is specifically a post-Christian paganism and as such is formed in direct opposition to Christianity. John Milbank describes it in this way:

> This religion is not quite accurately described as 'neo-paganism', because it is an embracing of those elements of sacred violence in paganism which Christianity both exposed and refused, and of which

paganism, in its innocence, was only half aware. The secular episteme is a post-Christian paganism, something in the last analysis only defined, negatively, as a refusal of Christianity and the invention of 'Anti-Christianity'.[17]

Visser 't Hooft describes very well the extent to which the fascist philosophy of Adolf Hitler is an early and failed version of this post-Christian paganism.[18] Paul Tillich, writing in the context of fascism, and wanting also to celebrate the achievements of the modern secular age, issued what has become a terrible prophetic warning:

> Our period has opted for a secular world. That was a great and much needed decision. It gave consecration and holiness to our daily life and work. Yet it excluded those things for which religion stands: the feeling for the inexhaustible mystery of life, the grip of an ultimate meaning of existence, and the invincible power of an inexhaustible devotion. These things cannot be excluded. If we try to expel them in their divine images, they re-emerge in daemon images. Now, in the old age of our secular world, we have seen the most horrible manifestations of these daemonic images. We have looked more deeply into the mystery of evil than most generations before us; we have seen the unconditional devotion of millions to a satanic image; we feel our period's sickness unto death.[19]

While we must acknowledge that neo-paganism does not have to take the acute form that it did in the Nazi ideologies of our recent past, nevertheless, because it has emerged in such a form, it is important that we understand the main features of a thought form which has now re-emerged as a post-modern paradigm. Visser 't Hooft is convinced that in our century, Western civilisation consists of '...a debate between three forces: Christianity, scientific rationalism and neo-pagan vitalism', and although for a time it seemed as if scientific rationalism had taken the lead, neo-paganism is now the major contender with Christianity for the heart of Western civilisation.[20] What then are the main ingredients of this debate as it impacts our present civilisation?

The characteristics of neo-paganism

The emergence of post-modernity as a form of neo-paganism and the revelation that a modernity stripped of its Christian foundation acts as an important precursor to this process, is relevant in understanding the changes that have been taking place in the culture of the West for some time. Understanding the structure of neo-pagan thought is important in order to identify the nature of some of these changes. How then can we describe the main characteristics of neo-paganism?[21]

1. Neo-paganism denies the personal attributes of God. In denying that God has the kind of personal attributes that allow us to speak of Him as loving, judging, speaking, and even feeling joy and sorrow, neo-paganism instead speaks of the divine as somehow impersonal. For the Christian, the human encounter with the divine is characterised by the words of the Jewish thinker Martin Buber. It is the 'I – Thou' encounter. For the neo-pagan such encounter can only be thought of as an 'I – It' encounter. In such an 'I – It' engagement, the divine is never the creator, but is always in some sense the created. It can take two forms.

The first, and rather simple form, is that the 'It' in question is merely a creation of man himself, whether this be a sacramentalised technology, or even an ideology that is worshipped. As Jacques Ellul has noted in relation to both these phenomena:

> The modern western technical and scientific world is a sacral world.... It would seem at first sight, that technology is not susceptible of such sacralizing, since it is rational, mathematical and explicable at every point.... Nevertheless, the fact is that technology is felt by modern man as a sacred phenomenon.... All criticism of it brings down impassioned, outraged, and excessive reactions in addition to the panic it causes.[22]

And again:

> On May 3, 1961, Premier Khrushchev addressing himself to Abdel Nasser, said, 'I am warning you in all seriousness. I tell you that communism is sacred'... Communism has entered that invisible, intangible,

dreaded, and mysterious domain in which lightening and rainbows mature, and the Grand Master was attesting to that mutation.[23]

The second and more ancient form is to worship the created order itself, whether that be as a constituent, representative part of the creation, such as the spirit of a tree, rock or even a mountain, or whether it is to attempt a mystical encounter, possibly through meditation, with creation as a whole. The idea is not to understand that which is encountered, but to derive power from the encounter. Unfortunately, in attempting to extract power from an encounter with the impersonal, there is always the possibility, some would say inevitability, that the person becomes overwhelmed by the impersonal and so becomes in some way depersonalised. By contrast, the 'I - Thou' encounter seeks to enhance the person, to give them meaning within the created order, so that as they are helped to become autonomous persons they may be able to meet the impersonal forces of the universe with hope and courage.

2. Neo-paganism lays claim to a dogmatic tolerance. The approach of neo-paganism is not dependent on a single system, revelation or doctrine. On the contrary it is able to accommodate almost any belief within its generous boundaries. Such an accommodating spirit gives every appearance of tolerance. But in fact, on closer examination, it turns out to be a very limited tolerance. It is a tolerance that makes such a dogma of tolerance itself that our suspicions are naturally aroused.

The apparent tolerance of neo-paganism is accompanied by an insistence on relativism. No belief is absolutely true, it can only ever be relatively or subjectively true. It might be true, (even absolutely so) for you, but not for the rest of humankind. In such a framework there is no universal truth, only an infinite number of approximations of the truth. Once again such a pluralistic approach gives every appearance of an attractive tolerance and even humility. However, it actually masks the very attitude it claims to abhor. As Newbigin states it:

The statement that there are no absolutes in history is obviously a pure assertion for which no proof is offered or can be offered. It is simply one of the axioms of our contemporary Western culture. It is pure unsupported dogma.[24]

The dogma lies in the absolute statement that there are no absolute statements! Much the same process takes place in the neo-pagan stance that all religious ideas can be tolerated save that one idea which claims for itself the status of ultimate revelation, especially if, as in the case of Christianity, that claim is rooted in a particular historical event from which all other events can be understood. In other words there is an implicit denial of the possibility of any transcendence in religious experience. Religious experience in neo-paganism is only ever an extreme form of immanence. So, revelation is never universal and located in historical events, it is only ever to the individual and in the present.

3. Neo-paganism identifies God and nature.   This is not quite the same thing as identifying God solely with nature, as a crude pantheism since, as we have seen, the object of man's labours can also be worshipped. But it does come very close to such a statement. The claim of neo-paganism is that it is legitimate to worship the created order. This must be seen in part as a reaction to the years of domination by a mechanistic, scientific world-view which saw nature as an adversary to be conquered by any means possible. But there is a difference between an appreciation of the value and dignity of the natural world, and a surrender to it as mystical, magical and powerful.

In some ways the social Darwinism of the nineteenth century laid the groundwork for such a view in that humankind was increasingly identified with the natural world. More recently the Darwinian overtones that *homo-sapiens* represents the high point in the natural order has been abandoned, to the point where some would see *homo-sapiens* as no more important or significant than any other species, and possibly as of less interest or value.

But even apart from such developments in science, the powerful themes of an encounter with the created order were present in European civilisation much earlier. During the eighteenth century,

Rousseau's thinking had increasingly contained a religious dimension. Such a development had arisen as a direct result of his own mystical encounter with Nature. Rousseau was by no means alone in his own generation. The art historian Kenneth Clarke has noted how there came a point in the Enlightenment period when there was an abrupt change in the way in which men looked at the natural world. For example, at one time the Alps were merely a barrier to be crossed. But at one particular period of time they became an object of beauty to be admired.[25]

Mankind was looking at Nature in a new way. He was concerned not just to understand and subdue it, but also to enjoy and appreciate it, to commune with nature. It is a short, though not a necessary step, to move from communion with Nature to a religious identification with Nature.

4. Neo-paganism seeks to intensify life rather than to transform it.
The concern of neo-paganism to celebrate the natural leads inevitably to a celebration of the life-force itself. Life has no moral purpose or meaning which would inspire an individual to work for the good of others. Rather, life is simply for living. Indeed the very purpose of life is understood as the act of living itself. Life is therefore an end in itself and so needs to be experienced ever more fully even if, paradoxically, the result of such intensity is death itself. The wild excess of youth culture is more than just an understandable testing of the boundaries; it is also an attempt to grasp life in order to understand it.

This does not mean that the neo-pagan cannot identify with a cause. Indeed the idea of the heroic and the noble is celebrated as a romantic embrace of the life force. The question of whether that cause is worthy of being followed is not as important as the involvement with an ideology for reasons of race, nationhood or some other demonstration of power. Even in the youth culture which transcends nationality there is a sense of a community seen as cult, sometimes sustained in the transcontinental community of electronic media. What matters in such a community is not the ideals of the cult. The act of belonging is sufficient to legitimise its existence. The issue of power is important because a celebration of the vitality of life tends to push life towards expressions which are uncontrolled. In any uncontrolled situation it is the most vital, or the most powerful, which will dominate at the expense of others.

5. Neo-paganism seeks to re-establish the place of Eros in its cele-bration of life.   The older pagan religions worshipped *Eros* in a very explicit way. The place of temple prostitution in the pre-Christian religions of Europe and the Middle East is well known. Neo-paganism seeks to re-emphasise *Eros*, not necessarily in a formal cultic ritual, although that too is not unknown, but more generally to see the experience of the erotic as somehow offering a means by which the life-force is grasped in a very immediate way. The presence of the pornographic element in modern literature is not simply a reaction to the myth of an earlier Victorian prohibition. Nor does it represent a mere response to the freedoms brought about by the possibilities of modern contraception to separate sexual encounter from procreation. It contains a definite religious dimension which seeks to see the sex act itself as an affirmation of self.

Ellul, along with others, has commented on the extent to which sex is regarded as an affirmation of autonomy and freedom:

> Anyone who performs a sexual act (even such a modest one as going to see Swedish films), however banal or however deviant the act may be, is looked upon as having achieved something. He has the sense of hav-ing shared in a great adventure. Never has sex been so glorified, so exalted, as when it has been made commonplace.[26]

And again:

> Sex becomes the manifestation of power. Sexual practices are more and more sophisticated, and sexual consumption becomes excessive.[27]

This identification of *Eros* as the sole content of love contrasts sharply with the Christian view that love cannot be understood without the inclusion of *Agape*, or love which contains an element of selfless giving and of commitment to the one who is loved. As

Visser 't Hooft comments, 'Eros is finally self-seeking and so its victories are often Pyrrhic; the victor does not reap any fruit of his victory.'[128] It is precisely the element of commitment in relationships that is so problematic for Western society today.

6. Neo-paganism is a religion without a definite, well-grounded hope. The twentieth century has been one in which there have been many false hopes. To a large extent, the present century was begun not in the year 1900 but in the year 1914 with the 'War to end all wars'. The false hopes of Communism, Fascism, and technology have proved so devastating in their consequences, that it would not be surprising if Western man deliberately opted to live without any hope at all. Lesslie Newbigin gives an account of his return to England in 1974 after many years spent living in India. He writes:

> In the subsequent years of ministry in England I have often been asked: 'What is the greatest difficulty you face in moving from India to England?' I have always answered: 'The disappearance of hope.'[129]

Yet the presence of a real hope is vital for a society if it is to remain healthy and not simply disintegrate into many private hopes which may even be more characterised by anxiety than genuine hope. What hope does neo-paganism offer in its search for an encounter with the life-force? As we have seen, neo-paganism seems to be more concerned with power than with establishing a basis of hope. It is as if only those who can grasp power can enjoy any hope. Yet such a hope speaks more of a response to anxiety than it does of a security founded on real hope.

The sense of a creation without hope is well expressed in the writings of the New Testament, which as well as acknowledging that an orphaned creation is without purpose or meaning, points to the real hope for which the creation itself eagerly longs:

> *All of creation waits with eager longing for God to reveal his children. For creation was condemned to lose its purpose, not of its own will, but because God willed it to be so. Yet there was the hope that creation itself would one day be set free from its slavery to decay and would*

share the glorious freedom of the children of God (Romans 8:19–21).

No power rooted in creation can bring that kind of hope. Only the Creator can legitimise that which he has brought into being.

The present religious impulse

The sources for describing neo-paganism stretch back to the end of the nineteenth century and before, as well as being present throughout the twentieth century. These themes can be found in sources as seemingly far apart as the literature of D.H. Lawrence and the philosophy of Nietzsche. And yet despite the fact that these elements have been present as important undercurrents for many years, it could be argued that what we have been describing is not something old, but rather the very contemporary phenomenon of New Age thinking. The similarities in thought are far from incidental.

There are some who point to the diversity of the New Age movement which embraces everything from Eastern mysticism to paganism, through to the occult, and conclude that it is not really one movement at all. Indeed there is a sense in which the term 'movement' is certainly a misnomer in that the varieties of religious experience are so great that as one observer has put it, 'it is unlikely that the participants in the New Age movement could organise breakfast together'. But such judgements are a little too hasty in dismissing a basic religious impulse which can attract tens of thousands of people to events such as Psychic Fairs and the like.

There is an important sense in which the nihilism of post-modernism, together with the older themes of neo-paganism, have helped to pave the way for the present religious impulse which often finds its expression in forms of New Ageism. Moreover these precursors also find a sympathetic echo in many New Age themes. It is important to recognise the points of similarity between all three approaches.

1. They are fundamentally ahistorical in their viewpoint. We have already seen that a post-modern perspective lives in the perpetual present with no sense of the past or of the future. Neo-paganism, in much the same way, is more concerned with the present than with the past or the future. For neo-pagan ideologies, the past is only there to be plundered for useful images and not for understanding the present. The future is only a glorious extension of the present. New Age thinking is dependent upon Eastern cyclical thinking. The past and the future are only different versions of the present. Both past and future are already found in the present since they are all inevitably to be endlessly repeated. However, New Age thinking gives the cyclical view of the East one additional twist by teaching that previous cycles or ages are in principle accessible in the present. So, according to one account of Shirley MacLaine's thinking, the past can be 'visualised' in the present in such a way that 'They are both now'.[30] The idea that the world had a definite beginning and is proceeding towards a particular end forms no part of any New Age thinking.

2. Truth is relative.   A commitment to the idea that all truth is relative and that absolute truths are unknowable or non-existent is widely shared by each of these thought patterns. In New Age thought, as with post-modernism and neo-paganism, there is no such thing as revelation in history. Knowledge has only to do with consciousness and as such is radically subjective. In such thinking two completely contradictory statements can both be simultaneously true. Any apparent contradiction is only a matter of individual consciousness. True knowledge is therefore to be found in self-realisation and not in knowledge of an objective physical universe.

3. Immanence is emphasised in opposition to the transcendence of God.   If God exists at all, it is as a force contained within the physical universe and not as a being who exists in any sense as independent of the created order. The radicality of this view of immanence is such that many who embrace it are actually advocating a form of atheism in the Western sense of that word. It is man who is the truly divine if he can find the key to his own divinity. There is a strong similarity between Nietzsche and New Age thought at this point. The created order can help mankind to discover his own divinity, thus there is no essential contradiction between the idea that man is divine and the concept that he can find his divinity partly through an encounter with the elemental forces of the world which he inhabits. The idea that 'I and the universe are one' is commonplace in New Age thought.

4. The role of Eros is important.   We have already seen the place of *Eros* in neo-paganism. Although not central to Hindu and Bhuddist practice, Vishal Mangalwadi has traced in some detail the extent to which *Eros*, represented by Trantric sexual practices, is an integral part of much New Age spirituality. He notes that in Trantic thinking:

> When the creator and the creation are perceived as one, not only is creation worshipped as divine, but also the procreative process – sex – is worshipped. Sex is logically looked upon as a possible key to unlock the mysteries of the universe.[31]

Not only is sex important in relation to knowledge, it is also important to assist the process of self-realisation. It is this aspect of Trantic practice that came to the West through the influence of those such as the late Bhagwan Rajneesh.

5. Power is more important than service.   The implication of Nietzsche's work leads to a glorification of power for its own sake. The supreme reality is the will of man as superman to have power over the elements. Milbank has argued that post-modernism not only always reduces the concept of freedom to one of power, but is actually grounded in an ontology of violence.[32] New Age thinking is also concerned with power but turns to magic, mysticism and spiritism to add to what it sees as the natural power of man. These spirit guides are in any case a creation of a person's higher consciousness. The apparently supernatural is harnessed to allow humankind to have power over the natural. Such a view stands in stark contrast to the Christian view which always seeks to make unnecessary the power of magicians, sorcerers and witches because it seeks to demonstrate a greater power, one which sees ultimate power as lying in the realm of sacrifice and service. The power of the crucified Christ, the very denial of power, is seen as the revelation of the true nature of God. Such a concept is unknown in nihilism, neo-paganism and New Ageism.

6. *The experiential is more important than reason.* For post-modernism, neo-paganism and New Ageism, reason is always suspect to some degree. That is not to say that any of these movements advocate irrationality, but all see the need to press beyond reason to experiential truth. In part this is a reaction to what has been seen as an over-reliance on reason in Western thought which can be characterised as an almost superstitious faith in reason found in modernism. But it is more than a reaction. It is making very large claims about the nature of knowledge. At a fundamental level, knowledge has to be experienced to be true.

Such a view stands in stark contrast to the Christian tradition which gives reason a very high value indeed. The claim of the Bible is that God is not capricious, changing or even insane, but a rational, loving Creator who has made the world in such a way that it does make sense, it can be comprehended. As Einstein commented, 'The most incomprehensible thing about the universe is that it is comprehensible.'[133] That paradox points the way, not to a suspension of reason, but to an accompaniment of reason with wonder. That sense of wonder stands at the heart of Christian worship.

7. *There is no ethical dimension.* It is strongly implied by much neo-pagan and post-modern thinking that those who survive because they are the fittest, somehow have earned the moral right to exercise power. The idea that 'might is right' is clearly very different from the older ethical tradition of Christianity. It points to the fact that there is no strong ethical content in these movements. Milbank describes post-modernism as ethical nihilism.[134] Similarly, Mangalwadi points to the absence of moral restraint in New Age thinking:

> In her own case, the karmic experiences of previous incarnations lead Ms MacLaine to the beds of many married men, with no notion that adultery is morally evil. Spirits and their channels confirm to her that in these love affairs she is working out the karma of her previous lives.[135]

The reasoning behind such behaviour is also explained:

> Chris, who puts Ms MacLaine in touch with her higher self, instructs her that every soul chooses the incarnation it gets. If a child is abused, he 'has to take the responsibility for his fate...his soul intuitively knows that he can't legitimately blame the parent for his situation, whatever it might be. A damaged child chooses to experience that.[36]

8. They are militantly anti-Christian.   There are two fundamental reasons why these movements are so strongly opposed to Christianity. The first is the very obvious point that they have all emerged in the shadow of the steeple.[37] At a very deep level, they are aware that many of the perspectives that they advocate are ones which were part of an earlier pre-Christian paganism. But that pre-Christian paganism was a more naive and gentler affair. The contact with Christianity was not for the most part a violent one. Although it is true that some Christians were martyred for their new faith and that in medieval times Christians in their turn persecuted others, for the most part such outright combat did not characterise the relationship between the older paganism and Christianity. But the new forms that the opponents of Christianity have taken have been shaped partly in reaction to the Christian faith. They therefore contain an implicit, as well as an explicit, defence against Christian thinking.

Secondly, they are aware that their thinking cannot colonise the Christian faith. The content of their thinking so fundamentally opposes Christian ideas that Christianity has to be opposed and, if possible, defeated if these new religious impulses are to feel safe.

This process then brings us full circle to the crisis of our culture. We cannot avoid the fact that Western culture has been significantly shaped in its past by Christianity. The challenge of the perpetual present introduced by post-modernism and the new religious impulse is not just that it introduces some new religious ideas. The task for these movements is much more radical. They seek to refound Western culture entirely. The jury is still out as to whether or not that is really possible and, if it is, what a future totally unconnected to our past, would look like.

CHAPTER FOUR

THE TEARING OF THE SOUL

Apart from the catalyst of overwhelming catastrophe, change in any culture is a gradual process. World-views change slowly, as do belief systems and patterns of commitment. Change, when it does come, might seem to be sweeping and powerful, but often the process of change has been operating gradually in unseen ways for many years. The redefinition of our culture sought by some has not yet taken place, but what we can see is a Western culture marked by considerable diversity. It is very rarely the case that the majority in any community are unmistakably neo-pagan, post-modernists, members of a New Age movement, or indeed anything else for that matter. But in the midst of gradual change there is usually a mixture of influences to be found. These influences are more often felt than measured, apprehended in something that we recognise rather than clearly defined in a single organisation or event. So what do these changes in belief and unbelief actually feel like when we meet them amongst those we know?

Present tensions

It is clearly very difficult to measure the precise strength and significance of what I have called 'the new religious impulse', although it is possible to gain some indication of actual involvement in some of the newer religious movements. For example, the anthropologist, David Burnett, has conducted some research on the numbers of people involved in neo-paganism in Britain. He quotes the Occult Census as indicating that neo-pagans are divided into

46% who practise paganism, 42% who practise various forms of witchcraft, and just 4% who engage in satanism. Burnett offers the following numerical estimate:

> In 1989, the Occult Census reported a 'conservative estimated population of 250,000 Witches/Pagans throughout the UK and many more hundreds of thousands of people with a serious interest in Astrology, Alternative Healing Techniques and Psychic Powers.' These figures would appear to be somewhat inflated from the observation of the various resources that would indicate a lower figure of no more than 100,000, but having many fringe members.[1]

These figures need to be seen in the context of an adult population of some 34 million people in the UK. In addition to these kinds of numbers, the researcher and sociologist, Eileen Barker, claims that as many as 1,000,000 Britons have been involved at one time or another in one of the many new religious movements that have come to Britain, often from the East via California.[2] But she also makes the point that most of these commitments have been rather short term and even in some cases formed part of the process of youthful rebellion and search for self-identity. Other information sources claim that there are more registered mediums and witches in both France and Italy than there are Roman Catholic priests.

Apart from the issue of the actual number of people who are involved in some kind of formal and structured commitment to one or other of the ingredients in this 'new religious impulse', there is the secondary question of the extent to which such an impulse influences more general modes of thinking and behaviour. Evidence is hard to come by. There are those who make the claim that New Age teaching has penetrated areas such as management training. It is frequently claimed that some companies conduct recruitment on the basis of graphology and other similar practices with little or no proven scientific content. But even if such claims are true, how significant are such developments? Is it the case that the dominant world-view of the West is rapidly being abandoned, or is it the case that it is actually remarkably intact but that there is some softness around the edges of the world-view endorsed by modernity? A recent article in the British newspaper, *The Times,* made the following claim:

> Sales of herbal medicines have risen by 70 per cent in the past five years, the fastest rise in Europe, according to a study by the market research group Datamonitor. Sales of homeopathic medicines have doubled in that time... The rapid growth is attributed to increasing disenchantment with orthodox medicine, which, although scoring spectacular successes against serious illness, has failed to make an impact on less severe chronic ailments. In a recent *Which*? survey, one in four people said they had visited an alternative practitioner in the previous year, twice as many as recorded in a 1986 *Which*? survey.[3]

What is the significance of such a report? Does it mean that a large percentage of the British population have abandoned the world-view of modernity, or is it only that the confidence of some has been sufficiently shaken that they are willing to experiment around the edges of that world-view? After all, the practitioners of orthodox medicine do not seem to be signalling that they are on the verge of widespread redundancy!

There are good reasons for thinking that the institutional structures of modernity, politics, science, capitalism, the universities, and technology (including modern medicine), are not about to collapse. All of these areas invest heavily in each other and in some senses depend on each other for the maintenance of their very considerable power. The very same edition of the newspaper quoted above also notes the discovery of a 'disease gene',[4] a discovery made by a team of scientists working internationally in the medical departments of a number of universities. The team's work has great potential for future development by the pharmaceutical industry.

The power of such institutions helps us to understand something of the puzzle in which our present Western culture is framed. The perspective of the broadcasters described in the first chapter of this book, who saw religion as something which belonged on the margins of society, was shaped by the structures of modernity in which they were educated. In taking such a stance, they reflect very well the opinions of their own professors and teachers, whose horizons were themselves formed at a time when the assumptions of modernity reigned unchallenged. It takes a long time for the questions of those who see the difficulties of the present world-view to become the new orthodoxy and then for that view to be mediated through the structures of society. Yet those who were schooled in modernity and who currently operate the levers of power, whether in the media or elsewhere, are aware that there are contemporary challenges to such views, but for the most part are unsure about how to handle such apparent contradictions.

This situation is further complicated by the fact that there is something of a transition of power taking place in many institutions today. The generation which was schooled in modernity and which shared its assumptions is gradually giving way to the generation of those who were teenagers during the 1960s. I would suggest that this particular generation feels the contradiction of the tension between the confidence of modernity and its failings particularly acutely. On the one hand this generation rejoiced in the freedoms brought about by an increasingly secular society but, on the other hand, began to experiment with a religious dimension in new and unexpected ways. They were schooled in modernity and its 'certainties' but in terms of their own youth culture embraced much that was in fact inimical to those same assumptions.

One example of the confusion caused by such tensions can be found in the offices and studios of a local radio station that I visited recently. The station in question has a potential audience of 1.2 million people. The ownership of the station changed a few years before my visit. The person who is responsible for the religious output of the station initially found that the new owners seemed rather hostile to the idea of religious broadcasting but, at the same time, the audience figures made them reluctant to axe the religious items. The correspondence received by the station regularly reflects the popularity of its religious output. The one religious programme broadcast each week attracts far more letters than all of the other output of the station combined. There is genuine puzzlement in the station over this state of affairs. The received wisdom of the broadcasters suggests that this simply shouldn't be happening. Religion, especially the Christian religion, which is the main content of the religious programming, ought not to be attracting such interest, yet it does.

Jonathan Sacks sums up such perplexing realities when he says:

> For some reason, religious conviction in the modern world produces in us a mixture of surprise, fascination and fright, as if a dinosaur had lumbered into life and stumbled univited into a cocktail party.[5]

The fact that such fright should now be occasioned represents perhaps the most unexpected development within contemporary Western culture. The growth of religious fundamentalism lives side by side with the faith of modernity which was so recently confident that all religions had been conquered. To quote Sacks once more:

> Marx and Freud had called religion an illusion. But now religion could reply that it had rejected the greatest illusion of modern times: the self-perfectibility of man. Precisely those religious movements that seemed to have been left behind by modernity became, ironically, an avante garde of post-modernity.[6]

The very word 'fundamentalism' often invokes images of fear, of holy wars and of religious intolerance. The reality is not always so frightening. But what is more important is the very fact that the emergence of fundamentalism, together with many other rather diverse religious responses, should have produced such surprise at all. At the macro level it illustrates how misplaced was the confidence placed in modernity. At the micro level it demonstrates how little we actually know about what people believe and think.

The anatomy of unbelief

The word 'unbeliever' presents us with something of a problem. As we have already observed, those who characterise themselves as 'unbelievers' do not believe in nothing. On the contrary, they often have a very definite set of beliefs which may well be held just as passionately as so called 'believers' hold to the tenets of their faith.

What then does someone mean when they use the word 'unbeliever' to describe themselves?

The word 'unbelief' has a technical meaning which dates back to its usage by Plato. In Plato's thinking, it was necessary for the good of society that certain theological beliefs should be widely accepted. For Plato, the necessity of such beliefs was so important that he suggested that failure to believe in such intellectual constructs should lead to certain punishments, namely, five years solitary confinement for a first offence, and death for a second offence. Thus, in the first instance, unbelief was simply and only a failure to believe in the basic theological ideas proposed by Plato, and as such said more about one's relationship to society than about one's encounter with God.[7]

This rather technical understanding of belief, and so of unbelief, is entirely alien to the world of the Bible. From a biblical perspective, unbelief is not a question of intellectual debate so much as a description of where one puts one's faith. Unbelief is not a failure to embrace religion so much as a rejection of the god of all creation. In the biblical sense, the highly religious followers of the god of Baal were 'unbelievers' because they failed to place their trust in the God who was first revealed by Abraham and later by Moses.

In both these very different understandings of the nature of unbelief, the notion of unbelief is defined or understood in relation to belief. It is not an entity that stands apart from the notion of belief. Therefore, there is a very important sense in which belief and unbelief are intimately connected. The one hardly makes sense without the other.

Both the platonic and the biblical understanding of belief and unbelief have continued in the popular usage of these terms throughout the history of the West. For example, Voltaire was very anxious to keep his own unbelief and that of his friends, within a narrow social circle. As Sacks puts it, he '...used to refuse to let his friends discuss atheism in front of the servants.'[8]. Unbelief needed to be reserved for 'consenting individuals in private'. He wanted his servants, his wife, and the serving stratum of society to continue to believe so that social order could be maintained. In taking what seems to us to be a strange and even hypocritical position, he was drawing very heavily on the platonic use of the term unbelief. The idea of theological belief, and by extension, of religion being used as a means of social control clearly emerges both in Marx and in much current political debate on the far right.

That other, more biblical usage of the term 'unbelief' as something which implies a different set of religious commitments, rather than no religious commitment, is also in evidence throughout the development of the West. The late sixteenth century saw the publication of many books written against atheism. But what was meant in many of these treatises was not the failure to believe in God, so much as a rather different belief in God. So, it was not uncommon for Anabaptists to be described as atheists, a description which might surprise their contemporary descendants in the various Baptist denominations![9]

The popular view of unbelief

The rise of modernity and secularism has further complicated the usage of the terms 'belief' and 'unbelief'. The thinkers of the eighteenth-century Enlightenment helped to break the earlier platonic and biblical connection between the idea of God and the idea of morality.[10] While the term 'unbelief' has never entirely lost these two earlier meanings, it has come to be associated much more with two other ideas. First, the categorical rejection of a personal belief in God, and secondly, of a personal distancing from institutional religious forms.

In the first case, it is sometimes possible to apply the religious terminology of conversion to those who dramatically throw off all belief in God. It is notable how those who take such a radical stance have often had a significant involvement in religious life before their conversion to atheism. Diderot himself, the great eighteenth-century atheist, had once aspired to the priesthood. He had wished to become a Jesuit and underwent a period of extreme religious asceticism, sleeping on straw, fasting regularly and even wearing a hairshirt.

Such examples of reaction are perhaps not as common as those who fit more easily into the second category. That is to say, some people have their own private beliefs which they perceive as standing outside of formal religious expressions or institutions. It is not that they have no religious belief so much, as the fact that they have their own personal system of belief which is sufficiently different from the traditional patterns of religious institutions and belief that they characterise themselves as 'unbelievers'.

The sociologist Thomas Luckmann makes the point that when sociologists investigate belief and unbelief they are using the categories mediated to them by what he calls religious specialisation. He suggests that this might not be a valid methodology for those industrial societies where there is a fracturing of the relationship between religious specialisation together with its concomitant perceived belief system, and the ways in which individuals perceive their own significance.[11] Commenting on current views of the secularisation thesis, the sociologist Steve Bruce has noted '...we have to build our general explanations of secularisation on a more detailed knowledge of religious belief and behaviour than we have at present.'[12]

Both Bruce and Luckmann are making a very important point. Our detailed knowledge of what it is that unbelievers actually believe is at best deeply flawed. In the second section of this book we will be making some general observations on the kind of data on beliefs and values that is available. But before we move to that part of the debate it is important to set it in the context of some appreciation of what so-called 'unbelief' actually feels and looks like. In terms of the popular meaning of unbelief, we know that there are few zealots for the cause of atheism. Far more people who think of themselves as unbelievers do so, either because they are unsure of what they believe, or because they see their beliefs as fundamentally private. Can we know what this private world of belief and unbelief is really like?

Everyday man

In the early 1970s I was studying theology at Birmingham University and also training to be a minister in a nonconformist denomination. Part of my training involved weekend preaching appointments in nearby churches. One particular church that students often visited was located in the Hillfields area of Coventry. It was and still is a red-light district with many of the attendant problems of social deprivation, drug abuse and crime. The congregation that nestled in the midst of the surrounding high-rise housing was very small in number. The number of surrounding unbelievers seemed to be astonishingly high when compared with the believers in church. This church, like many others, felt itself to be under siege.

On one particularly cold day I preached to just three people, all members of the same family. The husband led the service, his wife sat in the congregation and his son played the organ. It was not the high spot of a student's training! On that bleak occasion the leader of the church told me of a remarkable letter that had arrived from the United States. A team of young college graduates was going to come and work as missionaries at the church on a full time basis. Frankly I didn't think that this arrangement would work. What could a group of inexperienced Americans from the Midwest accomplish when everything else that the denomination had attempted in Hillfields had failed?

Eventually the team came and began their work. To my amazement the church started to grow. Many young men and women, often from the immediate neighbourhood, started attending and became committed Christians. Before too long the small building was full to overflowing and an extension was added. Over the years I came to know the members of the team together with some of their key converts. The leader of the team, Roger Edrington, was confident that any church in Britain could grow if they applied the same kind of methods that the team had used in Coventry.

My initial scepticism was greatly tempered by this evidence, but I did wonder if their experience had been unique. While they were seeing such success in Coventry, I was finishing my final year of training which included serving for a year as the student pastor of a small church in Erdington, a suburb in the north of Birmingham. The church that I worked in had an attendance that averaged around twelve people. Numerical growth was not part of our experience.

At the end of my one year pastorate I knew that I was unlikely to be replaced and was concerned that the church should receive some further help. I knew that Roger Edrington had been thinking of splitting the original team in Coventry into two teams, and I wondered whether Roger would consider coming to Erdington to lead one of the teams there. Eventually that is what happened. His arrival involved some jokes at his expense. Henceforth he was often introduced as Edrington of Erdington.

Roger had hoped to repeat the team's experience in Coventry. But that is not what happened. Certainly there was some growth. But unlike the situation in Hillfields where a good number of working class young men had joined the church, the working men of Erdington seemed absolutely impervious to the gospel message. This disturbed Roger because it was precisely these kind of men that represented a strong motivation in terms of his ministry commitment. Why were these men in Erdington apparently so resistant to the Christian gospel?

Research into the mind-set of the unbeliever

By this time I was studying for a Ph.D with the Professor of Mission at Birmingham University. Roger wondered whether it might be possible for him to study the particular issue of 'unbelief' in such a context. Perhaps such a study would give him some clues about the mindset of those he was working with. What was already clear was that Roger's particular experience and motivation in seeking to communicate with working class men equipped him in a very special way to conduct this kind of research. He cared about these men. He deeply respected them, and perhaps even more importantly, he had learned how to listen to them.

We talked together before he went to see the Professor of Mission. We particularly talked about the critical issue of the boundaries of the research. Roger was concerned with the total phenomenon of unbelief. I knew from my own experience of research that the precise topic would need to be much more limited than that. Eventually the topic was agreed and given the working title of the 'Mind of the Unbeliever in Erdington'. At first sight the parameters seemed rather limited given the very expansive concerns that Roger began with. However, the data that this research has provided is very useful in understanding the private world of unbelief.[113] Three observations seem to me to be supported by this data.

1. Good actions are more important than right belief.   Edrington's randomly chosen sample included 56% who described themselves as believers, 24% as agnostics, and the remaining 20% as atheists or unbelievers (p62f).[114] The figures are remarkably consistent with other surveys of the attitudes of the general English population. These chosen self-descriptions are themselves fascinating. For example, only a very few of the sample actually attended a church on a regular basis, or described themselves as in some way committed believers. Some 10% actually attended a church on a weekly basis. Four out of these five attenders were Roman Catholics. This finding is not surprising in that Erdington is known as a strongly Roman Catholic area with a high percentage of Irish immigrants having settled in that area many years earlier. A further 18% attended church occasionally, which usually meant only two or three times a year. Yet, curiously, 72% were happy to describe themselves as Christians. Used in this way, the term 'Christian' had little to do with membership of a church in any active sense. Rather, it tended to mean that they saw their actions as defining themselves as 'good Christians'. For the most part it was not intended as any kind of statement of belief.[115] Belief therefore was an essentially private matter and actions, unrelated to any institutional form of religion, gave content to their self-understanding.

2. Religion is intensely private.   Edrington's data reveals that the practice of prayer crossed the boundaries of belief and unbelief. It was not the case that the believers prayed and the unbelievers did not pray, although certainly there was a greater incidence of the practise of prayer amongst those who described themselves as believers. Some believers did not pray, some agnostics and unbelievers did pray. Even some who described themselves as atheists indicated that they occasionally prayed. At least one in this latter group felt that he could point to some specific benefits when he prayed.

Perhaps understandably prayer was seen as an intensely private activity. As Edrington puts it:

> For these men prayer was the ultimate in privacy of religion. Their wives often did not know that their husbands prayed and they, in turn, would not ask if their wives prayed....The place of prayer, therefore, became not the church but the private 'prayer closet', for one, at least theoretically, the water closet.[16]

The feeling that religion was a rather private matter extended to two other areas covered by Edrington's research. The first is that of religious experience by itself. As with the experience of prayer, there are no simple divisions on the basis that believers have religious experiences and unbelievers do not. Indeed one man described an experience where a 'fluffy angel' landed on his hand. But as Edrington says of this man's experience, '...it did not push him over the edge of his scepticism to actually trust God "because I haven't really had enough experience."'[17]

The second area is that of their conversation with others on religious matters. The general response was that matters of religion were never discussed with friends, workmates or family. Religion, together with politics, was a taboo subject. The only occasions when religion seemed to arise as a topic of conversation was when those who were considered to be 'religious freaks' raised the matter. The context in which this comment was made suggested that only those who were 'coloureds' ever raised this kind of issue.[18] Religion was not only taboo as a subject, it was also a matter of embarrassment. As with prayer, it was something that was kept hidden, even from wives. As Edrington comments, 'Even sex seems to be more openly discussed (and practised) than religion.'[19]

3. The church constitutes a 'world apart'.   As one might expect, the institutional church did not receive a good press. 72% of those interviewed had not attended a church since childhood. This is a significant finding because it also seems that the religious views of many, especially those who considered themselves to be atheists, were largely formed before they became adults. Yet it was not always the case that these men were actively hostile to the church in the sense that they had a bitterly remembered bad experience of the church, although a few could recount such experiences. It was much more that they simply could not imagine what possible use the church actually was. Edrington's description of the views of one particular man perhaps speaks for many of the others when he notes:

> More typical of the replies was the expected, 'I don't believe that you have to be a churchgoer to have belief.' He had never been to any church service on a Sunday in his life, yet he termed himself a believer and a Christian and spoke of, 'A faith such as ours', seeming to refer to the expectedly outworn 'Christian nation' concept. Speaking of his workmates, he added a comment which relates to many of the men, 'We all believe but don't participate.'[20]

The lack of participation is an important key because Edrington's data seems to agree with David Martin's finding that working class people are resistant to major involvement in any voluntary association.[21] The distance produced by non-participation produces some paradoxical attitudes. For the most part those who are uninvolved find the rituals of the church to be unintelligible but yet do not want the church to change. They want the church to be present but do not want to contribute anything to help it to survive.

The ache of isolation

The picture painted by Edrington is not therefore one of a conscious and considered rejection of active faith. Nor is it the case that many, if any, of these men can be described easily as secularists, postmodernists, neo-pagans or even less as New-Agers. But clearly the background of these various influences in the broader landscape of Western culture have undeniably had a considerable impact on the way in which these people live their lives.

The people described above include men that I have known through many years of work in similar areas. More interestingly, whenever I describe such men, even to very diverse audiences, there are almost always some who tell me that I have accurately described their husband, their father, their brother or indeed, even themselves prior to a profound conversion experience.

The overall picture seems to be of people for whom deep religious faith and conviction is simply not an option. It is as if their upbringing, their education, their experience of working class subculture as lived out in the pubs and clubs of working class life, their nominal affiliation to trade unionism, their experiences of the workplace, all convey a certain message. That message seems to be one of a reality in which there are almost no experiences of transcendence. The physical world is all that there is. That which one can see, touch, taste, feel and smell seems to sum up the boundaries of a life lived in isolation from others. Belief in any kind of afterlife is extremely limited. The attitude, 'When you're dead, you're dead', seems to sum up the lack of any hope in any meaningful experience of transcendence.[22]

Hope seems to consist almost entirely in maintaining one's individual health and relationships within a fairly limited circle of family and friends. There is some small feeling for class solidarity, but this does not consist of any hope that the working classes as a whole will somehow find liberation and political power, so much as just a strong sense that one is working class in background and values. If there is a God at all he is somehow very distant. Religion in any organised sense is seen as something that provides comfort. But that comfort is for women and children and for those few men who are so weak that they cannot manage without the crutch of religious involvement.

Just occasionally there seems to emerge the sense that there might be something more than the merely physical. It is almost as if the existential encounter of people with the world occasionally suggests a religious dimension, but a knowledge of how to express such feelings is absent. In any case, it is as if the emergence of such feelings must at all costs be denied and suppressed, kept so firmly within the realm of the private that such longings dare not be admitted even to those few people with whom one shares some intimacy – one's friends, one's lover, one's wife.

The picture that emerges is of people who are truly lost. They do not feel themselves to be valued. Their opinions are thought to be unimportant, unheard and unwanted. They cannot think with hope of the future but only of living day to day. The lack of value that they feel strips them of the will and ability to communicate, except perhaps within the family. They are silenced, and in that silencing lose both their ability to contribute and something of their dignity as humans.

It is as if such people live with an intolerable tension. On the one hand they are taught to believe that the world is a lonely, empty place. On the other hand there are occasional suspicions that this might not be true. But what does one do with such suspicions? The conflict between this taught world of the primacy of the immediate and their existential longings produces what can only be described as a tearing of the soul. Those who have worked amongst such people and who have shared their anguish, especially their anguish at funerals and at other moments of loss, will have felt this tearing of the soul. They will know too that terrible things can enter at the point of that tearing. Spiritism, the occult, the neo-pagan stand ready to enter at the point of the torn soul, not to heal but to heighten the fear.

It may be that such tension and loss is felt more acutely amongst working class people than it is amongst those who might think of themselves as part of the middle classes. Certainly we do not find exactly the same sense of being inarticulate amongst middle class men and women. Indeed one might almost say that it is the ability of the middle classes to ensure that their opinions are heard that marks them out as middle class. Although, even articulate middle class men appear to become strangely quiet when issues of religion, which many feel to be deeply personal, begin to emerge. But that does not mean that all is well in this difficult area of the tension between ones taught world view and a person's existential encounter with the world. Simply consigning such important issues to the arena of the deeply personal – so personal that one cannot ever speak about such matters – even to oneself, is no solution. Certainly there are those for whom this tension does not exist at all. There are those who are zealots for atheism just as there are those who are religious zealots. For such as these there does not seem to be any tension at all.

But as I have already suggested, the zealots amongst us are relatively few in number. Many others will have felt the depth of the question that my children and the children of my friends have asked, 'Where was I before I was born?' They do not wish to be told that they were simply in the womb. It is not a lesson in biology that they are seeking. The question is more meaningful than that. An adult can restate the question as, 'Did I exist, at least in principle, before I was ever conceived?' This question, and many others with it, can be suppressed and remain unasked and unanswered at a conscious level. But at a deeper level these questions do not disappear. Occasionally there come triggers which allow them to surface. When such triggers operate, we see the pain of these past tensions released in a way that allows that anguish to have some expression.

It is clear that for many older people in Western society, the experience of war helped to push religious questions further into the subconscious. It seems as if war experiences were so painful, or at least so far removed from ordinary life, that it has been difficult for many men to integrate those experiences with the everyday business of family life and civilian employment. Yet, in facing such dangers, such extremes of life and death, profoundly religious questions emerged, many of which were unanswered at the time. We can only know of such buried tension when an occasional trigger causes such feelings to emerge.

Very recently, for one man at least, such a trigger operated through the television screen in his home. The pictures were of the recent conflict in the Gulf. At the time of the Gulf war, when the Western allies were confronting Iraq in the desert of Kuwait, our television screens were often full of images of desert warfare. Apart from the aerial bombardment and the guns of distant artillery, desert warfare means tank warfare. The images of tanks hurtling across the desert sands evoked long buried memories for many who had taken part in the earlier desert warfare of the Second World War. One of those who participated in that North African conflict wrote a column in a Sunday newspaper in which he described what he experienced almost half a century ago. He described what took place following one particular battle:

The next day we went out to the road to recover what Italian tanks we could. There was a smell of burning flesh amid the smouldering ruins. Men were dropping off the tanks with their legs blackened and these dropped off when we pulled the bodies free. Heaps of gooey black stuff were inside the tanks and these heaps had been men. It was a sight that I shall never forget and I know that my soul will be damned for having been a part of it.[23]

That article speaks not just about the pain of war, which is undoubtedly present. There is also a deeper anguish present. It is the feeling 'that my soul will be damned for ever for having been a part of it.' That sense of damnation, and so of isolation, speaks for the many who though articulate in the ordinary course of life and living, feel somehow robbed of the ability to say anything about the great matters of belief and unbelief which confront us at an existential level. The silenced men of Edrington's study speak for a larger community. They help us not just to understand the problem of unbelief, but to feel it.

CHAPTER FIVE

BELIEF OUTSIDE OF THE CHRISTIAN COMMUNITY

Believers and unbelievers do not live in entirely different worlds. The impact of the culture is felt by all who live within that culture. In that sense the problem of unbelief, or of how to believe and what to believe, is an issue that affects everyone, believers and unbelievers alike.[1] Moreover, the particular religious history of the West is such that it is never entirely clear who it is that is an unbeliever and who it is that is a believer. The terms believer and unbeliever are used in a variety of ways depending on who is using them and in what situation.

Defining believers and unbelievers

We began to see something of the difficulty of using the term unbeliever in the previous chapter. Unbeliever in what, believer in what? Certainly there are those people whose self-designation is that they do not believe, by which they mean they do not believe in God, in religion in general and the Christian religion in particular. But, as Edrington's research shows, those who describe themselves as unbelievers do not believe nothing about religion. Some pray and even see answers to prayer. I have met clergy who wished they had more church members like that!

To make matters even more complicated, some who call themselves unbelievers happily identify themselves as Christians! Used in this way the term 'Christian' comes to mean someone who acts in a moral way, a good person. Still others are happy to call themselves 'a religious person' but never or rarely attend a church and have only a very hazy idea of what it is that they believe about anything of a religious nature. In stark contrast, some who are very active Christians reject the idea that they are 'a religious person' because some Christians see that term as carrying very negative connotations. What a confusing situation!

Are there more objective criteria that we can use to give some meaning to the word unbeliever? The two most used measures of commitment to particular beliefs are those of membership and attendance. But the question of membership is more complex than one might imagine. There is a huge gap between the memberships that churches report that they have and the numbers of people in the general population who report that they belong to a particular denomination.

The various denominations attach rather different meanings to the concept of membership. For example, the definition of membership in some denominations is sufficiently strict that only a small number of those who regularly attend would actually be a church member. The Church of England has traditionally taken the number of Easter communicants to be their membership, but more recently the electoral roll has taken precedence in terms of assessing the strength of a particular church. (At least one Diocese in the Church of England still uses the actual population of each parish as the basis for calculating the parish quotas – a partial throwback to the time when everyone in a community could be assumed to be part of the parish church). Increasingly, the financial pressures on denominations have led to local churches keeping their membership figures as low as possible in order to avoid a very high assessment of what they should be paying into the denominational coffers.

The figure given by MARC Europe for church membership in 1990 indicated that 15% of the UK population was a church member. However, when pollsters ask the public whether they belong to a church and if so which one, a figure closer to 65% is usually given in the UK. The discrepancy between these two figures is so enormous that it is abundantly clear that a perceived (even if not actual) affiliation to a particular church carries a strong cultural as much as a belief content. Some 37% of the population in England considers themselves to be Anglican and 10% Roman Catholic. The size of this gap is far from being unique to Britain. It seems to be a feature of the Western world. For example, in New Zealand, the 1991 government census reported that 73% of the population considered that they were affiliated to a church. In Italy in 1990, the figure was 58% of the population and in Canada, in 1993, a staggering 91% identified themselves as belonging to a Christian church of one kind or another. The churches in all these countries would be delighted to see such numbers in attendance!

The believing 'unbeliever'.   If the concept of church membership carries conflicting messages, is the category of church attendance any more helpful? It doesn't take much imagination to realise that the idea that all who attend church are believers and all those who do not attend are 'unbelievers' would be both untrue and offensive to many. And here we find a clue to one of the key difficulties with the word 'unbeliever'. It is a word which is far from neutral in its meaning. It can carry great emotional content. While the term unbeliever might be worn with pride and honour by some, it can just as easily be perceived as a self-righteous and unjustified slur on their character by others.

Despite this difficulty, recent research indicates that there are marked and identifiable differences of belief between those who attend church at least once a month and those who rarely if ever attend church. The differences between these two groups brings us back to the rather more classical meaning of the term 'unbeliever'. In the situation of the West, whose cultural heritage has been the Christian faith, an unbeliever is not someone who does not believe in God, nor is it a term of abuse, it simply describes someone who has chosen to step outside of the Christian tradition either to express an informal faith or to celebrate having no particular religious faith. Therefore, for the purposes of this study, it is this narrower and rather technical meaning of the word 'unbeliever' that we are going to use – someone who is detached from the Christian community in the sense that they no longer have any active contact with the Christian community or with any other identifiable formal religious structure.

Patterns of belief and unbelief

Throughout this book there has been an attempt to speak not just about the United Kingdom, (although there is a bias in such a direction), not just about Western Europe, but about the situation of the West as a whole. Such an attempt is fraught with difficulties as others have also discovered – not least because of the complexity of the nations that constitute the civilisation which we call 'the West'. The term 'the West' is not a geographical description except in a very loose sense. Rather, it describes a culture which has common roots and a common inspiration. But within that common culture there are vastly different histories and experiences. The religious history of the United States is particularly different from that of the rest of the West. As Francis Tyrrell puts it:

> The United States constitutes an odd, if not unique, phenomenon on the religious landscape of the Western world. We puzzle the Europeans and even defy our own self analysis.[2]

Amongst the nations of Western Europe, Ireland too, both North and South, is unique in terms of the astonishing survival of community religion. Because of these very different histories and cultural peculiarities, each country in the West produces slightly different figures for church attendance and for church membership. The strength of particular denominations varies enormously from country to country and even within individual countries on a regional basis. These variations are so great that even if such a survey existed, it is doubtful that a single survey which asked the same questions would produce a useful aggregate picture of what the whole population of the West believes. But what is clear from the various surveys that do exist is that whatever the variations in the precise numbers of people in each country who believe one thing as opposed to another, there are some very similar underlying patterns across the whole of the West.

It is these patterns rather than the precise statistics that should excite our attention. For example, it does not help us much to know that 58% of the population in Italy claim to be affiliated to a church compared with 65% in the UK, or 73% in New Zealand. But what is important to note is that the figure for church affiliation is both consistently high across the West and also that it is gradually decreasing in virtually every Western nation. In other words, the pattern is more significant than the precise statistic in each country. It is these patterns that we will consider in the remainder of this chapter.

In order to engage in the detail which will be necessary to understand something of the differences of belief between those who regularly attend church and those who do not, I am drawing on some research which has been specifically commissioned for the purposes of this study. The study was carried out during 1993 by a professional researcher amongst a sample group of 1484 respondents, each of whom were asked some very detailed questions about their beliefs, attitudes and values. Those who were surveyed were asked whether they attended church at least once a month, at least once a year, or whether they attended less often than once a year/never. These groups are referred to later in this chapter as Group 1 (attending once a month), Group 2 (attending once a year), and Group 3 (attending almost never). The responses given to the survey were compared and contrasted between these three groups and written up in a report called the British Values Study (BVS). Some clear patterns emerge from this research.

There is a relationship between the British Value Study and another governmental study known as the European Values Study (EVS).[3] This enables us to check some of the findings of the commissioned research with a wider study and also to gain some sense of whether the patterns that are detected carry a wider resonance with the whole situation of the West.

The features of belief and unbelief

1. Unbelief as belief in an impersonal God. Jonathan Sacks, the Chief Rabbi of the United Hebrew Congregations of the British Commonwealth, who gave the Reith Lectures in 1990, chose as his title for his lectures the phrase, *The Persistence of Faith*. Sacks described the way in which the various faith communities in the Western world have been able to maintain and develop their traditions of committed belief in the face of the onslaught of modernity. He comments, 'Instead and against all prediction, religion has resurfaced in the public domain.'[4] If faith in this committed sense has proved to be persistent, then belief in the existence of some kind of God is even more surprisingly prevalent in the Western world.

As we look at the populations of a variety of Western countries from Europe to the Americas through to the Antipodes, there is a surprisingly high level of agreement that there is some kind of God. Certainly the figures vary a little, but even in the most secular countries, including those where church attendance is the lowest, (around 1.5% in the case of Denmark), large majorities seem to agree with the proposition that God does exist.[5] But we have to ask the question, what is the nature of this belief or, what kind of God is believed in?

The Christian tradition clearly teaches that God is not just an impersonal life-force or spirit, but is above all a being who can be described as personal. The biblical view is that man has been created in the image of God and is capable of a personal knowledge of and relationship with God. As one might expect, the belief in God as a personal God is very widespread amongst those who attend church at least once a month. 67% of those in this group (Group 1) conceive of God in this very traditional Christian formulation. The contrast between this group and the two groups who either attend church once a year (Group 2) or rarely if ever (Group 3), is very marked. In these latter two groups the overwhelming view of God is that God is a life-force or spirit. 52% of those who attend once a year and 41% of those who rarely or never attend church see God in this way. Only 27% in Group 2 and 20% in Group 3 believe in a God who is personal.

What about those who aren't sure what they think? The number of 'don't knows' amongst the frequent attenders is almost insignificant. But once again it is relatively high and fairly consistent in the two remaining groups. Because of the number and nature of the alternative responses to this question, one can assume that there is a degree of openness both to the idea that there is a God and to a Christian understanding of that belief. To put it slightly crudely,

20% of those who never attend church display a broadly Christian understanding of God as a personal being in their framework of understanding, while a further 21% have not ruled out such a belief. In fact only 16% of those who never attend a church and only 5% of those who attend once a year would say that there is no God or spirit/life-force. No one who attends church at least once a month disbelieves in the existence of some kind of God. Unbelief in any kind of God is very much a minority position across all three groups.

The beliefs of non-churchgoers and occasional church attenders about God are strongly echoed by their attitudes towards the importance of God in their lives. On a scale of 1–10 with 1 indicating that God is not at all important in their lives and 10 indicating that God is very important in their lives, the average scores came out as follows. Frequent attenders, 8.02; those who attend at least once a year, 5.67; and those who rarely or never attend, 3.93. The detailed statistics reveal that there are significant numbers amongst those who never or who rarely attend church for whom God is very important. It may be that there is some correlation between those who do not attend but see God as personal, and those in the same group who see God as important in their lives.

2. Unbelief as adherence to folk religion. What do we mean by the term 'folk religion'?[6] Folk religion can be described as a syncretistic mixture of religious belief with superstition. Usually folk religion in any given situation draws on the predominant religious tradition in the culture for some of its ideas, but infuses a memory of those traditional beliefs with a range of other beliefs and practices which are in clear opposition to the major tradition. So, for example, a belief in God is not seen as inconsistent with the reading of horoscopes. The idea of chance or even of 'good luck', can easily be confused with prayer to the Almighty. Traditional religious rites are more associated with protection against the malign forces of the elements than they are with joining a community of faith. In such a framework, the baptising of infants is not a first step to joining the church, as much as it is a divine insurance policy designed to ensure that a baby does not suffer from 'bad luck' or even the evil eye. In folk religion the graveyard that surrounds a church may well have more significance than the communion serving rail.

It is an understanding of the word 'religion' as more often meaning 'folk religion' that causes some Christians to reject so strongly the idea that they are a 'religious person'. The use of the term 'religious' illustrates some aspects of folk religion. The British Values Survey finds that 12% of those who attend church regularly reject the idea that they are a religious person, whereas 67% of those in Group 2 and 36% of those in Group 3 would describe themselves as a religious person, even though their attendance at church is either occasional or non-existent.

The prevalence of an approach to belief as 'folk religion' is well illustrated by the perception of those in groups 2 and 3 of the need for religious services to mark the 'rites of passage' (birth, marriage and death). So, for example, 76% of those in Group 3 said that it was important for death to be marked by a religious service. 69% of the same group felt that marriage should be marked by a religious service, while a majority (55%) felt the same need for a religious service to mark the occasion of birth.

3. Unbelief as indifference to the church.   This view of the role of the church as important for the rites of passage stands in stark contrast to the way in which those in Group 3 view the general relevance of the church. Only 18% of those in Group 3 saw the church as giving adequate answers to moral problems and the needs of the individual. The same percentage thought that the church was helpful in relation to the problems of family life and even fewer people in Group 3 (16%) saw the church giving adequate answers in the area of social problems. These relatively low scores for the relevance of the church given by Group 3 are markedly different to the views of those who attend church at least once a month (Group 1). 56% of regular attenders saw the church as giving adequate answers in the area of moral problems. 63% felt the same about the church in relation to family problems, while Group 1 respondents were at least three times as likely (49%) as those in Group 3 (16%) to express confidence in the church in the area of social need.

Not surprisingly, given this generally low view of the relevance of the church to everyday life, those in Group 3 expressed very little confidence in the church as an institution. Only 7% recorded 'a great deal' of confidence in the church as an institution and only 17% would say that they had even 'quite a lot' of confidence. 55% had 'not very much' confidence and 20% 'none at all' in the church. So, whereas there is little confidence in either the relevance of the church in society or in its standing as an institution, its role as helping in the rites of passage is seen much more positively by those who rarely, if ever, attend.

4. Unbelief as belief without formal content.   The consequence of belief outside of any community of faith is a high degree of uncertainty about what it is that is believed. We have already seen that amongst those who only occasionally or who rarely attend, God is more often conceived of as a life-force rather than as a personal being. But the incidence of belief in some kind of God is quite high. 56% of those who rarely, if ever, attend church claim to believe in God. But the content of that belief is less clear when specific religious issues are raised. So, for example, when questions are asked about belief in the afterlife, a wide range of responses are received. Indeed the answers might even seem to be a little confusing. 40% in this group claim to believe in heaven, but only 31% in an afterlife. Slightly fewer people in Group 3 believe in a traditional Christian doctrine such as the resurrection of the dead (18%), than believe in the Eastern religious idea of reincarnation, (20%).

The same kind of patterns emerge in relation to other traditional Christian doctrines. Belief in the existence of the Devil in Group 3 is low (20%), and the same pattern is repeated with regard to the concept of Hell (16%). Such responses contrast sharply with declared beliefs in religious concepts which are not as strongly connected with traditional Christian doctrine. Thus, 54% in the same group believe that there is such a thing as the soul. In other words, it is not that there is no belief amongst those who rarely, if ever, attend church, it is just that the content of that belief is rather diffuse and generalised in its expression. Interestingly the beliefs which attract very little adherence amongst non-churchgoers are also beliefs which are not held to as strongly even by those who do attend church. It is likely that Western culture as whole has made it very difficult to adhere to certain Christian doctrines and that such adherence is a problem for both churchgoers and non-churchgoers alike. However, the fact of regular church attendance has the not unexpected effect of strengthening traditional teaching.

5. *Unbelief as belief for emergency use only.*   We have commented on Edrington's observation that unbelievers do pray on occasion. The British Values Study seems to confirm his findings. According to this survey 37% of those who rarely or never attend church pray on occasion. But the circumstances in which people pray is revealing. Almost half of those in Group 3 who do pray say that they pray only in times of crisis. Only 11% say that they pray often.

One might ask why it is that people who have a very tenuous connection with any kind of formal religion pray at all? The dominant response in Edrington's work seems to indicate that those who call themselves unbelievers pray for one of two major reasons. Either prayer provides a sense of well-being, or there is a clear claim that it seems to work. In either case it is the utilitarian value of prayer that is important rather than any sense that it is an integrated part of an active knowledge of God. Seen in this way, prayer is not necessarily valuable for its own sake, (as part of a religious response to life), so much as useful for what it does.

6. *Unbelief as belief without belonging.*   The fact that belief in God is widespread amongst non-churchgoers and that God is somehow important to many of those same people, together with the view that the church is important in terms of the 'rites of passage' but irrelevant in other ways, gives rise to the sense that there does exist a subliminal faith which might be described as 'belief without belonging'. Something of the character of such belief is revealed in two surveys, one conducted by The Bible Society in the mid-1980s and another by the researcher Rosalie Osmond.[7] Both of these surveys were carried out with the help of the Gallup organisation. In both cases they reveal very similar

attitudes to one other key element in the religious tradition of the West – the Bible.

These surveys reveal a high level of Bible ownership (8 out of 10 homes in England) and relatively high numbers of people who claim either to read the Bible occasionally, or in emergencies. They display a surprisingly high regard for the value of the Bible.[8] While it is certainly true that regular church attendance has a significant effect on the extent to which people read the Bible on a regular basis, and also on which versions of the Bible are owned, there is a widespread agreement that the Bible is a positive influence in peoples' lives. Yet when those same people are asked other questions designed to discover what they know about the content of the Bible there is a high degree of ignorance, not just about detailed content, but about almost anything.

Rosalie Osmond's research indicates that very few people can quote anything from the Bible by memory. Nor is this lack of knowledge confined to the Bible itself. It seems that few people can display much knowledge of anything connected with Christian worship.[9] No matter whether it is liturgy, hymnody, creeds or prayers, few can recount with any degree of certainty the content of these elements which represent part of belonging to the community of faith.

Does this lack of immediate knowledge really matter? The point about the Bible and the other elements of Christian worship is that these are the means by which the content of the Christian faith have traditionally been transmitted. Indeed some have argued that many in the past knew more about Christian doctrine through the words of hymns than they did from the efforts of preachers. The lack of belonging by itself erodes the content of belief. Belief without belonging leads to belief which has very little content and so ultimately to belief without meaning.

The memory of faith in the unbeliever

Unbelief is not so much the conscious rejection of faith as it is the continuance of a belief which is increasingly unconnected with a living religious tradition. We can describe unbelief more as the 'memory of faith' than as the embracing of atheism. The concept of the memory of faith connects belief and unbelief and helps to explain something of the mixture of these two elements in the present religious landscape of the Western world. Five features of the topography of such a landscape seem to be very prevalent.

1. The past is more important than the present.   Christian faith is identified with the idea of a Christian heritage, with values that society once held, with childhood, with the memory of school assemblies and with a very ill-defined memory of what constitutes Christian worship. The great cathedrals in our cities and ancient village churches are important because they preserve something of that common past. There is often a greater concern about the prospect of an ancient church building being closed amongst those who never attend the church than amongst those who do. Many vicars have told me that they have more problems with schemes to reorder the church building from non-attenders than from attenders. The Prayer Book service known before liturgical reform, the Authorised Version of the Bible as somehow the 'proper' Bible, these and other distant memories are all valued much more by those who do not attend church than by those who do.

Coupled with this concern for the externals of a past faith is the sense that Christianity is somehow linked to the preservation of a 'high' culture from the past. Fine music, beautiful words and a sense of the aesthetic value of religion are much more important as the preservation of the achievements of the past than any expectation that Christianity will make a dynamic and creative contribution to contemporary culture.

The question of the West's connection with its memory of Christianity is an important one. Os Guinness quotes the writer Jaroslav Pelikan as pointing out that, 'There is all the difference in the world between tradition as the living faith of the dead and traditionalism as the dead faith of the living.'[10] Later in the same section he comments, 'Jews sometimes say of the modern Jewish community that no generation of Jews knows more about the past, yet is less a part of it.'[11] A past which is only a distant memory and plays no significant part in the present cannot offer any resource with which to illuminate the future.

2. Faith as an alien culture. The evidence that emerges from the work of MARC Europe indicates that in Britain the active Christian community is declining but is also becoming more committed. Leaner but fitter is the phrase borrowed from the language of recession to describe this process. In part this development reflects the gradual emergence of evangelicals as the driving force in the life of the church in the West. It also reflects the fact that church attendance is not as socially acceptable as it once was. Becoming an active and committed Christian requires a much stronger decision to live at odds with society's norms than it once did. This process carries with it the danger of creating ghettos. What has certainly begun to happen is a tendency for a cultural gulf to emerge between those who believe in an active sense and those who believe but don't belong.

Writing in the *Independent on Sunday*, William Leith describes a visit to his local Anglican church to witness a christening service:

> Will anybody spot me? It's like when you're in a strip club: you think, with relief, well, if they do spot me, they're in here too. Organised religion has sunk pretty low these days, at least among people I know; the feeling is that it's just third-raters who get involved, oily little tinpot careerists or neurotics, people afraid of the modern world...This is my local church, these mild-looking people must be my neighbours, but I've never seen any of them before; religious people and pagans live in completely different worlds these days. A ritual is being organised, quite a frightening one, with people standing in formation around the central focal point, the ... altar, and, my God! Someone's carrying a baby towards them! My tabloid-conditioned satanic abuse needle gives a jolt... At the end, I'm bolting for the door, pushing a bit, unable to help myself.... Outside the church, the noisy, irreligious world looks great.[12]

No doubt Leith's tongue was firmly fixed in his cheek, (did he really kneel down and pray that God wouldn't get him, as his byline suggests?). But apart from risking the wrath of those who had invited him to attend the christening of their child, he reflects fairly well something of the feeling that marks the gulf between committed faith and a more obtuse form of generalised belief.

3. Faith as residual rather than active.   Those who have led marriage services and funerals where a large number of those present have clearly not attended church in the recent past, will know something of the embarrassed half attempts to sing the hymns and to follow the events of the liturgy. The greetings at the door of the church are often accompanied by an avoidance of any eye contact. There is much looking at the floor and/feet shuffling with an awkward unease by those who wait to exit the church.

Yet conversations with those same embarrassed spectators after the event, perhaps at a wedding reception, reveal much more. There are very few who argue for a full-blooded atheism. Instead there is evidence of a half-remembered distant faith. Some speak of a time when they did have a stronger contact with a church of some description. They tell of what they would like the church to be without any desire to participate to bring about such perceived change.

Curiously, the church that some describe as their ideal is in fact much closer to what those who are part of the church know that it has become. But the points of contact between that residual memory and the actual Christian community are sparse indeed. The content of residual faith is actually very close to what Christians believe, but the gulf of human contact has become almost unbridgeable. There seems to be a division, not between believers and atheists, or even agnostics, but between knowledgeable participants and what some have called 'ignostics' – those who can't remember what faith consists of rather than those who have rejected faith.[13]

4. Faith as a leisure pursuit.   Lack of time rather than lack of faith is frequently cited as a reason for not attending a church. But what lies behind such a statement is not actually the overwhelming busyness of people, so much as the perception that a commitment to faith and worship is not sufficiently important to warrant giving up time to be involved. Viewed in this way, church membership and church attendance is simply an option that some people take in the way that others might make time to be involved in a running club or in some other social club or voluntary organisation.

Those who attend church might be viewed with a mixture of curiosity and gratitude. Curiosity because it seems like such an odd activity to spend so much time on. After all it seems to be a very demanding leisure pursuit because it makes demands not just on the actual time spent in worship, but on the living of life outside of 'club' activities. Gratitude because the involvement of the few ensures that the many do not need to be involved in order to keep the facilities of the church open to all for occasional use. It is not that most people would wish to condemn those who worship as practising something which is completely false so much as investing time in something that seems to be so marginal. It is not so much untrue as unimportant.

5. *Faith as opposition to change.*   When faith is a memory of how things were and of values which are treasured rather than argued for, then adherence to a vaguely Christian culture can also be a reluctance to see change more widely in society. So, changes in the wider culture, especially in the area of family and sexuality, are resisted on the basis that traditional values are best, even if it is difficult to say precisely why this is so. Of course, when values cannot be argued for on a clear intellectual basis, then change does come, but only gradually, and ground is given grudgingly. But it is almost impossible to resist even those changes which are felt to be undesirable even if those who have such feelings are not able to articulate why they are undesirable.

In a British context, people are rarely so sure that they are Christians as when they feel themselves to be overwhelmed by people from another strong faith position. The arrival of large immigrant communities from Muslim lands ensures that many indigenous populations wish to assert their Christian culture, even though they have no real understanding of the content of that faith and have not attended any Christian worship for many years. In such a situation, to be Christian merely means not to be Muslim.

The future of faith

Clearly, when faith is only that which is remembered and is no longer personal and active, then its future is highly questionable. It almost certainly is difficult to transmit the memory of faith to future generations. Memories are important but they need a living context in order to have meaning for those who have no firsthand contact with faith. They have to matter in order to be worth transmitting.

On the day that these words are written, the news media have reported the release of an Iranian Christian who had been sentenced to death as a punishment for converting from Islam to Christianity. His life was saved, but he had spent ten years in prison for his beliefs. Although there are many active Christians in the West who might be willing to withstand persecution for the sake of their faith should such a thing ever be necessary, it is difficult to imagine anyone whose contact with faith is only that of memory being willing to undergo such hardship. The notion that religious belief might be important enough to die for, or to be martyred for, is completely outside of the framework of reference of most in the Western world.

CHAPTER SIX

DISTANT MEMORIES OF FAITH

The framework or content of beliefs held by any society inevitably affects the structure of morality that a society adopts. This is not to suggest that only people with a strong religious faith can have a strong moral basis for their actions, while those who call themselves unbelievers do not. It is only to raise the issue that differences in belief structure are likely to influence beliefs about morality. Indeed there is not a necessary connection between a specific religious belief and any system of ethics.

It was one of the features of the Old Testament tradition that it made an explicit connection between faith and ethical behaviour, that the worshippers of the God of Israel were seen as distinctly different from some of the nature religions that surrounded the nation of Israel. This inheritance has caused the Western tradition to think in terms of the linkage between morality and faith, but it is, of course, perfectly possible for those who are not believers in any particular religious faith to hold to a clear ethical framework. But whether we call ourselves believers or not, the changes that are impacting the Western world are so significant that all ethical systems are currently undergoing a significant testing.

The impact of change

The speed of change, so graphically surveyed by Alvin Toffler and encapsulated in his phrase, 'future shock',[1] is perhaps not as important as the nature of the changes that developments in technology bring into the arena of human possibilities and choice.

None of these developments are more fundamental than the complex web of discoveries which raise questions about life and death itself. Man has always had the possibility of ending life – his own life, the lives of others – but never before the twentieth century has there been the possibility of ending, not just many lives, but all of life – human, animal and plant life. Even apart from the threat of a nuclear holocaust, whether occasioned by the deliberate intent of mankind gone mad, or whether by some horrific misunderstanding or accident, there still remains the possibility of ecological disasters which may poison our planet, our only home, as effectively as a holocaust would end it.

Added to this global possibility of annihilation, there come many complex individual questions concerning life and death. Is it ever right to end the life of someone who is suffering? Do individuals have the right to decide when their life should be ended? Given that it is now possible to keep some systems of our bodies functioning even when the brain appears not to function, when is someone judged to be dead? When has life truly ended? Since some people could be cured of particular diseases but the cost of curing all would be prohibitive, how does one decide what constitutes a reasonable cost and who decides who should receive treatment and who should not?

Is it right to end the life of the unborn? Do the unborn have rights? If a foetus is aborted, is it right to use their genetic material to enhance or save the lives of others? Should the eggs of an aborted foetus be used as donor material in implantation techniques? Is it morally acceptable to allow parents to choose their children's characteristics? If it is right to choose some and not others, which would they be? Is it acceptable to choose hair and eye colour but not gender? Or is it permissible to choose gender but not to interfere with characteristics such as a homosexual orientation? Should we allow the cloning of human beings in the way that animals are now cloned? These are no longer tomorrow's questions or the preserve of the imagination of the authors of science fiction. Not only these questions but even more difficult, and at first sight horrific questions, are with us already.

Change, dramatic, far-reaching, both life-threatening and life-enhancing – is forcing itself upon us. We cannot wish it away. The social consequences of such change are dramatic. Some observers believe that the advent of the contraceptive pill was a decisive factor in producing a sexual revolution. In the words of one pundit of the time, sexual intercourse was only invented in the 1960s. Certainly the idea of sexual intercourse as primarily recreational rather than procreational features strongly in contemporary Western culture.

Changes in technology have not just brought challenges to personal and corporate morality, they have also brought huge changes to the human systems which had previously safeguarded, monitored and agreed on moral codes of behaviour. All over the West the rise of the individual has brought with it the loss of a sense of community. Margaret Thatcher's famous phrase, 'There is no such thing as society', was a philosophical and ideological point, but it is also an observation of that which has taken place in Western culture. The move from the countryside to the cities disrupted but did not end a sense of community. New communities were formed in the workplace, and even in the slums of the new cities. The strength of the new industrial communities, the miners, the shipworkers, the steelmakers and the factoryworkers, created new political as well as social realities.

But that landscape has now gone. Communities are now not so much places where people are known but only where they live. Increased mobility means that those we know and who know us might not necessarily live near us. Community is no longer a physical description so much as a social creation across many boundaries. In the absence of strong communities, the family assumes a new importance. The question as to whether it can bear the weight of such responsibility is one that we will consider later.

The question of relative values

The complexity of the moral dilemmas which face humanity, together with the erosion of the structures which might have faced such questions, is made even more complicated by the absence of a clear conviction about the existence of moral absolutes. Truth and morality are inextricably connected. But the advent of modernity has suggested that truth can only be arrived at with any certainty in the realm of the objective world of facts. Kant not only consigned religious belief to the realm of the subjective, morality also belongs in the same category.[2] In modernity the only absolute is the absence of absolutes. Truth, in the sense of truth about morality and ethics, is always relative. The extreme of such relativity is well expressed by Hemmingway: 'What is moral is what you feel good after, and what is immoral what you feel bad after'.[3]

Not only is the growth of relativity in values apparent, but so too is the emergence of society as essentially pluralistic. We no longer consist of a society composed of just one culture. There are now many different cultures, religions and races living side by side. Significant groups of people from other parts of the world have come to live in the West. There is not just one truth, there is a plurality of truth, of values and of morality. The advent of a plural society adds a new complexity.

The term 'pluralism' carries two quite different meanings. On the one hand, pluralism can suggest merely a further dimension of relativity – a further limiting of any absolute claims. On the other, it can mean quite the opposite, namely the competition of very different sets of absolute values.[4] The latter meaning is in fact closer to the actual meaning of the word pluralism, but the connection with a relativistic way of looking at the world is so strong that in the debate on values, 'plural' is used almost interchangeably with 'relative'.

Western values.   The reality of a changing, highly individual, relativistic and plural society provides the context in which the values of modernity are lived out. These are not everybody's values, but they are the values that inform and inspire the dominant institutions of the West, particularly the assumptions that form the political landscape. What are these values? In summary, the core values of Western society are:

the freedom and human rights of individuals;
the superiority of democracy over any other system of government;
the exercise of toleration;
the importance of equality.

Clearly these values are closely interrelated. The role of a democracy in expressing the views of the majority is not seen as violating the rights of those who become a minority. Toleration insists on the right of the minority to speak.

In actual practice there are some strange contradictions contained in the value system of the West. The rights of the individual are not balanced by any insistence on the duties of the individual. Nor is it always entirely clear what happens when the freedom of the individual clashes with the democratic view of the majority. Thus, freedom of thought and expression often comes to mean the freedom to think and practise whatever one likes in private, provided that it does not infringe the rights of others. But these boundaries are difficult to maintain. There is an assumption that private views do not affect the rest of society. In such a system, adults should be free to read, view or practice in private whatever they like. Debates about the effects of pornography and the practise of homosexuality revolve around this central question. Medieval society, (in common with some other societies in our world), maintained that duty is more important than rights, or at the very least, that rights need to be balanced by responsibilities to society. There is an argument which suggests that private behaviour and even private thinking cannot be separated from its effects on the rest of society.

The value of toleration is closely linked to a broadly liberal view of many public issues such as crime and punishment. At times this core value clashes with a commitment to democracy. So, for example, there has always existed a strong majority view in Britain that hanging should be reintroduced as part of the penal system. It is also clear that the House of Commons is not likely to reflect this majority view in the foreseeable future.

The toleration that is espoused is a toleration of a particular kind. It is a toleration which insists on the absolutising of relativity! So for example, one newspaper columnist in Britain described the commitment of their son to evangelical Christianity as the ultimate rebellion. The use of illegal drugs or other signs of rebellious youth they could have accepted, but to become a Christian represented the ultimate offence. I am aware of another parent who, when greeted with the news that their daughter had become a Christian, (in fact in an Anglican church), actually threw their offspring out of the house. In the view of the parent the action of their teenage child violated every principle of open questioning of everything that they had carefully taught. In this particular case it took many years to restore the relationship.

The combination of dramatic change, together with the challenge to the West which genuine pluralism has introduced, has further provoked an already developing cultural crisis. There is real anxiety concerning the basis of morality and values which is sometimes manifested in an advocacy of 'traditional values' or 'family values' without any clear definition of what such talk really means. In such a situation, common sense can come to mean no more than an extension of what I think is true.

A Christian heritage

Despite the fact that a commitment to an active involvement in the Christian community is a minority activity, and that many values in Western society flow from a secular viewpoint, these same values are very close to those of an older Christian inheritance. This is not altogether surprising in view of the claim made in earlier chapters that in many ways modernity was partly a product of the Christian faith. Even the highly central commitment of the West to a tradition of toleration is arguably one which flowed initially from the initiative of those Christians who stood outside of the major faith communities in Europe. Indeed, the society and values of the United States were strongly shaped by the aspirations of many groups who travelled to the New World in order to escape religious persecution enforced by the marriage between certain expressions of Christianity and the power of the State.

The experiences of the first Anabaptists (the forefathers of many Baptist groups) in Zurich, were not untypical of many Christians in Europe. In Zurich, it was the civil authorities and not clerics who decided that all of the children of Zurich would be baptised as children. Theological issues were inseparable from the issue of stability and order in society. The history of the West in the modern era is partly the story of establishing freedom for the voice of religious dissent. That struggle is inseparable from the subsequent commitment of the West to toleration. The story of that struggle for toleration was largely the story of Protestant Europe. It has only been in recent times that the same degree of commitment to a religious pluralism has become the norm in many Southern European countries.

But the growing tradition of toleration in the West, of a working pluralism in religious practice, did not bring a serious disagreement in the area of private and public morality. The broader Christian heritage and agreement as to what it means to be a moral person have remained the dominant inspiration of Western life, at least until very recently. The broad consensus that flowed from an earlier Christian heritage in Western society concerning the content of morality has experienced a very marked challenge in recent years.

Imposed moral values.   Some commentators believe that the first challenge to such a consensus came in the 1960s and centred on the debate about sexual ethics.[5] Significant changes in attitudes to sexual morals were accompanied by changes in legislation in the area of family law, censorship and abortion. Popular culture as reflected in the subject matter dealt with by television, theatre, the cinema and literature, both reflected and encouraged these dramatic changes in moral attitudes. While the challenge to traditional morality began with an attack on attitudes towards sex, it did not stop there. We are now familiar with the arrival of a hedonism in modern culture that defies all attempts to cite more traditional understandings of what constitutes morality.

Such developments have often been celebrated as the arrival of 'freedom'. Those individuals who have often been seen as the representatives of the new morality, pop stars, artists, actors and designers, have often spoken about the 1960s as a golden age when creativity was released as part of the new freedoms being demanded and won by the post-war generation. However, such freedom was essentially the freedom of the few. Not too many of those amongst the poor in the West experienced the new morality in quite the same way. Along with the new freedoms have also come soaring rates of drug abuse, high crime rates (partly fuelled by the demand for drugs), increased divorce rates and the growth of one parent families. It has often been the poor who have not only committed crime disproportionately to their numbers in the population, but who have also been the major victims of crime and other aspects of social disintegration. The rich are well insulated against the consequences of such trends.

The absence of moral values and teaching.   The breakdown of a consensus about the basis of morality is not likely to be easily reversed. Indeed it is never a possibility to return to older values as if the immediate past had not taken place. But why is there a need to have such a debate at all? Why is it not possible to simply accept that from now on morality will simply be a matter of individual choice in which the consensus view of society plays no part? The immediate stimulus for such a debate arises partly as a consequence of the signs of social disintegration mentioned above. At a very basic level, the new morality seems to have produced a society which simply does not work. There is a sense of alarm which focuses on particular events which happen to catch the attention of the public in ways that draw attention to what is perceived as a moral malaise. It may be a relatively minor event – the interview on television with a father who is proud of his son's achievements in crime, (largely the theft of cars), on a working class estate, because at least he is seen to be advancing his economic position. Or it may be an event which shocks a whole nation – the killing of a toddler by two young children. In the midst of a crisis of confidence about the present and the future, there is inevitably a degree of nostalgia for the past. But how does the memory of a better, more certain past, help?

The researcher Christie Davies has produced convincing figures from the UK to demonstrate the relationship between attendance at Sunday School and the incidence of crime.[6] The detail of the research documents that crime in the latter part of the nineteenth century fell as attendance at Sunday School rose. Conversely, as attendance fell in the twentieth century so crime rose. The basic thesis supported by the research maintains that the teaching of

Christian values produced a strong consensus as to what constituted moral behaviour. The weakening of that consensus resulted, in the words of Christie Davies, in a 'moral confusion', with the consequence that 'deviant behaviour' became a much stronger possibility.[7] But what lessons can be learnt from such research? It is extremely unlikely that any government will finance and encourage Sunday Schools as part of the fight against crime and the creation of a consensus about moral behaviour. Nor do the churches seem to have enough confidence or practical means to reproduce the strength of a previous era.

The strength of the Sunday School movement was just one expression of the vitality of strong Christian communities in society, a strength which owed much to an earlier and vibrant evangelical commitment. However much it might be demonstrated that a strong belief in God produces desirable social consequences, that by itself is not enough to encourage such belief. However, these findings do at least draw attention to the importance of a number of key debates which lie at the heart of any discussion of values and morality.

Key moral dilemmas

Is there then a consensus on morality between those who attend church and those who do not? Is the memory of a Christian past sufficient to produce such agreement or are there some irreconcilable differences in ethical judgements between believers and those who stand outside of any faith community? Two issues emerge as vital in arriving at a consensus on moral behaviour. First, is there such a thing as right and wrong, (meaning right and wrong actions) and secondly, can we begin to speak about the existence of good and evil (understood as the concepts which underlie right or wrong behaviour)?

In discussing both these questions it is clear that the memory of a Christian past does play some part in the debate. Whatever our stance in relation to the issue of faith, the filter of the past cannot be avoided. Two elements in that past feature strongly:

1. The Judaeo Christian tradition. The conclusion of Rosalie

Osmond's research on morality in Britain suggests that morality in a British context is Judaeo-Christian morality.[8] It is this historical framework that gives the word morality meaning. This reality can be seen most clearly when British people encounter a moral framework that stems from another tradition, for example, Islam, and find views on morality that substantially differ from the Judaeo-Christian tradition. It is not that other people's views are seen as immoral, but neither would they be recognised as part of the normative moral framework of the West.

2. Tradition as conscious or unconscious. Osmond further points out that the Judaeo-Christian framework inherited by society is an unconscious one and as such is much weaker than if it were conscious.[9] The implication of such a claim is that there is a very weak basis for maintaining a Christian ethical tradition in the face of a determined attempt to introduce another consistent and well-argued framework for morality. Some may have strong feelings about what they believe to be right or wrong without being able to say why this is so.

Given these two elements, how do people respond to the concept of right and wrong? A very high percentage of British people (68% of the whole population, 58% of non-churchgoers), believe that there is such a thing as sin. This is one traditional way of saying that some things are wrong. In this sense, there is a commitment, amongst churchgoers and non-churchgoers to the concept of right and wrong. But this general agreement obscures two rather different approaches to this issue. The first view believes that some things are wrong in a categorical sense. That is, there are some absolute values or standards which mean that certain actions are always right or always wrong. The second view maintains that right and wrong can only be determined on a circumstantial basis. That is, you can only know if something is right or wrong by taking the circumstances surrounding the action into account.

The statistics that emerge from both the European Values Survey (EVS) and the British Values Survey (BVS), cited in the previous chapter, indicates very clearly that churchgoers and non-churchgoers take strongly divergent views on this issue. Churchgoers are far more likely than non-churchgoers to hold that there are some absolute standards against which behaviour can be measured. Conversely, non-churchgoers are significantly more likely to believe the reverse. Within these two groups, those under 25 are even more likely to view right and wrong on the basis of circumstance. Rosalie Osmond has produced similar results and adds that those who have attended university, studied arts rather than science, and who are secular in their outlook, are almost certain to take a circumstantial view of morality.[10] As other researchers have noted, it is people from this latter group who tend to dominate the editorial decisions of the media and other institutions which influence opinion.

Despite this difference in approach, there is a broad agreement about the fact that there is such a thing as right and wrong behaviour and agreement as to the nature of what constitutes that behaviour. For example, murder and theft are largely regarded as wrong, both categorically and circumstantially.

However, when it comes to the question of the basis of morality, that is to say, the existence of some underlying view of good and evil, there is much more confusion. Once again, part of the problem attaches to the desire of many to say that circumstances play a large part in knowing where something is intrinsically good or evil. 30% of non-churchgoers in the BVS survey agreed that 'there are absolutely clear guidelines about what is good and evil', while 64% responded that 'there can never be absolutely clear guidelines about what is good and evil, as what is good and evil depends entirely upon the circumstances at the time.'

So if there is such a thing as right and wrong, but guidelines as to what is good and evil depend on circumstances, how do we arrive at a knowledge of how circumstances affect the issue? Even if we think that there are clear categorical guidelines, where do these come from? How are they learnt?

The overwhelming emphasis of all groups, whether churchgoers or not, is to look at the family as the place where norms of right and wrong are learnt. However, there are two other broad observations we can make in relation to this general rule. Those who are churchgoers, naturally enough, do see an important role for the church in moral guidance, both for morals more widely and for the conduct of family life. Those who are educated in church-related State schools, as compared with those educated in State schools with no church link, see the role of teachers and other figures, such as clergy, as fairly important, to such an extent that reliance on the family for guidance on morality drops substantially. There is no significant other source for guidance on morality cited by those who have little or no church contact other than the family. The importance of this difference is that those who see the value of sources other than the family as places where morality is both learnt and reinforced have some fall-back position in the event that the family, for whatever reason, fails as the transmitter of morality.

One possible conclusion from these findings is that whereas there is broad agreement on Christian values as the basis of morality, knowledge of what that morality actually is, and an agreement as to the principles that underlie it are much more tenuous. We do seem to be dealing here with memory, with families as the only safeguard of that memory. Moreover the large differences in the attitudes of those under twentyfive could indicate the imminent breakdown even of the consensus that does exist. The tenuous nature as to current understandings of the content of Christian morality begins to be illustrated when we look at how particular issues are viewed.

The application of morality

The existence of a common Judaeo-Christian tradition, whether remembered consciously or unconsciously, inevitably means that there are very similar attitudes exhibited by both churchgoers and non-churchgoers on a wide range of issues. On occasion, for example on abortion, the agreement that exists between these two groups seems to differ from the traditional, inherited Judaeo-Christian tradition. It is clear that in these instances the views of churchgoers have been significantly influenced by the views of society as a whole. Such instances illustrate the extent to which the memory of a past inheritance has been insufficient to act as a framework for moral decisions. But having indicated that there is a broad consensus in operation between these two groups, there are two areas of clear difference.

1. The exercise of honesty. There is no disagreement that personal honesty is a good thing, but when it seems as if the action is only a matter of personal choice and does not appear to harm others in a personal way, then there is a sharp divergence of view. So, for example, when the issue is something such as taking a car which does not belong to you, taking drugs, or killing someone in an extreme situation such as personal defence, the attitudes of the whole population do not differ very much. But in other more personal areas, for example, cheating the government of tax, avoiding the payment of fares, lying when it is in your interests to do so, buying something you know to be stolen, or even accepting a bribe, there are some very marked differences in attitude. In each of these cases of personal honesty, those who are churchgoers respond much more clearly than non-churchgoers that these actions are always wrong.

2. Sexual behaviour. On issues such as prostitution, 'having an affair', or practising homosexuality, once again, those who are church-goers hold much more traditional views than those who are not church-goers. There is a strongly utilitarian undercurrent in the views of those who are not regular church-goers. Thus there is the view that having an affair is not wrong in and of itself. It is only wrong when the fact of an affair seriously harms the well-being of those who are thought to be innocent parties. It is difficult to avoid the slightly cynical conclusion that the message would therefore seem to be something like, 'by all means have an affair, but if you are going to do so, don't get caught.'

These differences in attitude illustrate the moral dilemma for the modern Western world. On the one hand, the whole of Western society wishes to maintain a broadly Christian understanding of morality, but on the other there is increased uncertainty as to what the basis of that morality really is. The idea that Christian values depend, not just on circumstance, but on a categorical view of what good and evil really are, is experiencing a real challenge. The family and not the church is what undergirds such moral teaching. The evidence indicates that for many secular people families depend less on contact with the church for the maintenance of such values. Given that younger people have far less contact with the church than older generations, it is questionable whether future families will be able to maintain a broader Christian understanding of morality if such teaching depends only on what seems to be right in certain situations.

This same difficulty can be illustrated by looking at the connection with the teaching of the Christian minority in another way. A number of researchers have categorised the composition of churchgoers and non-churchgoers in a more detailed manner. They have pointed out that churchgoers can be understood as core members (those who attend at least once a month), modal members (those who attend occasionally), and marginal members (those who attend only once a year). Non-churchgoers can be divided into those who are first-generation unchurched and those who are at least second-generation unchurched. In terms of attitudes to moral issues, those who are modal and marginal church members tend to be markedly closer to the attitudes of those who are unchurched than they do to those who are core churchgoers. In other words, when it seems to be the case that the views of those who are not churchgoers are the views that are in the ascendancy in society as a whole, it is only those who are core members who strongly maintain a Christian view of morality as containing a categorical approach to issue of right and wrong, good and evil.

This contrasts sharply with those situations where the views of Christians are the driving force in society. In such a situation, not only are the views of modal and marginal churchgoers closer to the views of core churchgoers, but even the views of the first generation of unchurched are much closer to those of traditional Christian morality.

The sense of anxiety and even crisis of morality which is felt by Western society is therefore a genuine one. On the one hand there is a desire to uphold traditional values, especially as they relate to the family, but on the other hand there is a real question as to what the basis of such an appeal really is. The critique of Christian values which comes from the new morality is therefore very strong, even when at an emotional level there is a desire to resist such arguments.

Those who are unbelievers seem to pride themselves on the virtue of tolerance. The commitment to maintaining the rights of individuals to maintain a high degree of personal freedom can, nevertheless, conflict with a strong desire to uphold traditional moral values. The views of core churchgoers are often seen as being rather narrow-minded and are even presented as lacking in tolerance. Yet the very principles of those who are presented as narrow and intolerant are also the values that many would like society as a whole to maintain. There seems to be a contradiction between the desire to see others uphold Christian values and the determination to maintain a high degree of personal freedom to behave as one thinks fit. Politicians urge the church to preach about morality, but such preaching is greatly resented when it seems as if it might apply to the individual lives of those who publicly advocate such an approach.

This confusion might not matter a great deal in the context of a society which is not facing great change in the area of personal moral choice. But when the challenges facing society are as complex and as far-reaching as those that are outlined at the beginning of this chapter, one can only predict considerable conflict as to the future structure of society's values. A distant memory of a Christian past will not be enough to maintain a continuity with that past. In this sense, Western society is at something of a crossroads. It is a real question as to how the West will deal, not only with its own internal moral quandaries, but also with the critique of its morality from well-formed traditions, such as Islam, that come to it from outside of its own distant heritage.

That question also comes as a challenge to the Christian community. It is not enough for the Christian community to appeal to the past as a basis for morality. The contemporary value and application of a distinctly Christian morality needs to be argued on its own merits. The Christian community will need to take account of the vast technological and societal changes that are impacting the whole world community. This task should not be undertaken as a reaction to such change. The resources of the Christian past are considerable, varied and rich. There is some reason to think that a carefully considered response to the moral challenges of our age will receive a sympathetic rather than a hostile response from many who still live with an unconscious memory of their Christian past.

A quest for a vision of morality inevitably raises the question of a search for meaning. Such a search for meaning not only raises questions about the meaning of our own actions and relationships within society, but it also impinges very strongly on the question of the meaning of the whole of life. Where can we look for inspiration to answer these questions of morality and meaning?

CHAPTER SEVEN

BLOWING IN THE WIND

In the novel, *The Beautiful and the Damned*, two of Scott Fitzgerald's characters discuss whether life has any meaning. The dialogue includes the line, 'I don't care about truth. I want some happiness.'[1] Truth, meaning, morality, freedom and happiness, all are encompassed in the confrontation of Fitzgerald's characters. It is not by chance that all these elements are found in the same conversation, for there is an intimate connection between them all.

Are we really free, autonomous beings, or are we so conditioned by our environment, our culture, our genetic make-up and the happenings of chance, that any sense of freedom is largely illusory? There are very few who would argue in support of either of these extremes. Few imagine that we are entirely free beings, uninfluenced and unconstricted by a range of other factors. In this sense the 'superman' of Nietzsche has always been an illusion. But the idea that we are so conditioned by factors beyond our immediate control, to the point where we are doomed to play out our lives in ways that are entirely outside of our freedom to choose, attracts little real commitment either. Certainly the assumptions made by our culture, religious traditions and legal system insist that we do have some responsibility for our own actions. Indeed, the freedom to choose to act in a moral way is associated with the idea of human dignity. It is not freedom by itself that gives humanity dignity since freedom can be used to demean or degrade humanity. Freedom and the intent to choose the good constitutes that which bestows dignity. This idea underlies the notion of heroism which has been so powerful in many cultures and has certainly provided a rich seam in the literature and culture of the West. Yet even the idea of the heroic has been under severe attack in recent years, so much so that the anti-hero has often taken centre stage.

The supposed freedom to choose raises yet another question, 'on what basis do we choose?' Apart from the threatened sanction of the penal code, a sanction that many choose to ignore, why should we choose to do one thing rather than another? Do we only act out of pure self-interest, even if at times it can be presented as enlightened self-interest? Can our responses be understood only in terms of the kind of socialisation typical of our species – the naked ape syndrome? Or is there a morality which can be understood and used as a basis for individual choice and community behaviour?

One approach to morality is the appeal to conscience. The idea behind such an appeal suggests that there exists a natural human conscience which alone will lead free human beings to choose that which is good. But, as we saw in the previous chapter, there are those in the modern world who are deeply sceptical about the results of such an appeal. Some suggest that how one feels after one has acted informs a person as to whether the action was right or wrong. In other words, the elevation of freedom as a principle brings a potential crisis concerning the nature of truth. Is there any truth beyond the simple fact of how one feels? The appeal to feelings suggests that there is no universal truth, there is instead only the very local and temporary truth of feelings. Truth of this kind is merely personal, existential truth. In such a framework, the idea that there might be some kind of universal truth which is independent of feelings, stands in opposition to the idea of personal happiness, as if the existence of universal truths prevents us acting as we might truly wish – a kind of unseen tyrant. Hence the statement of Fitzgerald's character, 'I don't care about truth. I want some happiness.'

Such a debate about truth raises the related and very important question about life and its meaning. It causes us to ask the question, is there any meaning to life other than the meaning which we choose to give it? Yet the question of meaning is also crucial in relation to the quest for happiness. It is almost as if the human condition cries out for some sense of meaning and significance as part of the search for happiness and fulfilment. The explorations of the first few chapters of this book suggest that this issue is very central for modern man. The various forces which have shaped the modern and post-modern world in which Western man lives offer very different responses to the issue of the meaning of life.

The possibility of meaning

The Christian faith is unequivocal in its assertion that life has meaning and purpose. From Genesis through to Revelation, the purpose for which humankind has been created is made clear. Humankind has been made by the Creator as a companion, to know and worship God. In the words of the Westminster Confession, 'Man's chief end is to glorify God and enjoy him forever.' Humankind is given the very specific task of caring for the created world on God's behalf. He is to be a steward, a caretaker of the created order. The issue of morality, of man's relationship with his fellow man and with the created world, flow from this central declaration of the meaning or purpose of life.

However, as we have seen in the first few chapters of this book, this older Christian tradition, which ascribes a particular meaning to life, has been severely challenged by other understandings of this issue. There are many other responses in the Western world to this question. The following represent some of the major options which present themselves at a popular level.

1. Meaning does not come from outside of the human condition but only from the meaning that society chooses for itself. The major thrust of the secular tradition that comes to us, particularly from the social sciences, suggests that man has learnt to become autonomous. His autonomy is strengthened by means of his understanding the internal needs and drives of the human species and by describing the ways in which these internal needs are worked out in other social relationships. As mankind learns fully to understand this panorama, so he is able to come to terms with the meaning that is ascribed to himself by virtue of his nature as an independent being. So, for example, if one accepts a Marxist view of man's nature and of his relationship with others in society, one comes to accept that mankind finds meaning by acting in accord with that fundamental nature and by co-operating with the inevitable destiny towards which mankind is bound as a consequence. For the Marxist, the genius of Marx is not in deciding what man's meaning is, so much as in discovering the true nature of man and his social interaction and so of allowing individuals to choose to act in accordance with that true nature. Because it was claimed that Marx's findings had a scientific base (scientific socialism), to act morally in such a system is simply to choose to act 'scientifically'.

While the Marxist analysis of man's nature and societal patterns is perhaps more extreme and less flexible than many other systems of thought, the basic principle of deriving meaning, and thence morals, from the concept of a correct understanding of who man is, remains the same. Although the framework might be less dogmatic, the underlying commitment to an attempt to derive meaning from a correct 'scientific' analysis of mankind is a constant theme in secular thought.

2. The quest for meaning is simply an illusion – it does not exist.
Some observers of Russia in the 1990s have noticed how strongly superstitious many in the population seem to be. Faith healers, few of whom would attract much attention in the West, are given major air time on television. Charlatans abound and yet can easily attract an audience and a following. Is the real nature of the Russian soul reasserting itself in the post-communist situation? Some claim that the final years of the Communist regime were deeply marked by the presence of such phenomenon, not necessarily because Communism itself was collapsing and so allowing Russians to revert to their true nature, but more because Communism had for years paraded as scientific what everyone knew to be nonsense. Such public absurdity undermined confidence in anything that claimed to be scientific and has since driven people to find hope in the irrational.

By contrast, the West still seems to retain a certain confidence in science and technology; after all, the cold war with the Russians was won with a superior technology. But the supremacy of technological achievement carries with it the terrible price of the loss of individual human significance. We seem to be in a situation where we have more and more information without a corresponding means of making much sense of the increased information that we have.[2] As the cast-iron certainties of previous attempts to find meaning collapse, it is understandable that many should wish to conclude that all such attempts are futile. It is not that the systems at our disposal, (capitalism, communism or religion) are inadequate, but rather that they are all engaged in a hopeless quest. They fail simply and only because there is no meaning in life. The attempt to impose meaning on that which we see around us is just that, an imposition, which says more about the beliefs of those who construct the system than about life itself.

3. Meaning comes from our self-understanding as divine. Whereas secular thought tends to see the individual as having significance in relation to the society or even the species of which they are a part, the growing individualism in Western culture has also had the opposite effect in that the world is interpreted through the significance of the individual. The decade of the 1970s was often seen as one in which a new introspection began. The very decade itself became labelled as the 'Me, myself and I decade'. That concern for the self has sometimes been presented as a reaction to the world as a global village. The loss of new continents to explore and indeed the very ease of travel around the continents we now know well, as compared with the challenges and romantic allure of travel in previous ages, have left the journey inwards as the only significant adventure available to modern man.

These intriguing suggestions which attempt to explain the concern with self are not as important as the phenomenon itself. The radicality of a concern with self which attempts to give understanding to the world through self, implicitly leads to a deification of the self. We are the god whom we worship. This suggestion is made much more explicit in the various New Age philosophies which have abounded since the 1970s. Such thinking follows a fundamentally Eastern understanding of the self as potentially divine. The discovery of individual divinity allows one to have a knowledge of the nature of reality as an extension of a person's consciousness. Meaning comes through self-discovery and not by means of an exploration of the world around us.

4. Meaning comes from our encounter with life. The new religious impulse of our age takes many forms. The neo-paganism which is emerging in our century is not just one form, but manifests itself in many guises. But there is a commonality when it comes to the question of meaning. In one sense there is the same kind of pessimism that we find in the nihilistic conclusion that life has no meaning. But neo-paganism does not quite go in that direction. Instead it opts for a kind of vitalism, or energetic engagement with life, which suggests that our very encounter with life is what gives our life meaning.

There is something very attractive about such a bold and confident assertion. But there is also a dark side to this encounter. Deep within such approaches to life there is also contained a view of God as unknowable in any intimate way, but also as capricious and malicious. This God (or even gods), understood as spirit or life-force, is part of the malevolence of the universe. Therefore part of one's response to life is to be aware that these dark powers need to be assuaged, subdued to some extent, and even controlled. The gods, or the powers, must be dominated by man in order that he can use them for his own ends. Such domination is never entirely complete or certain, but the very uncertainty forms part of the vitality of engagement with life. Meaning is not therefore derived from rational understanding, it is intuitive, dynamic and experiential.

The popular perception of meaning

It is one thing to speak about the theoretical possibilities for a belief that life has some meaning, it is quite another to describe what people actually think. Both the European Values Survey and the British Values Survey asked a number of questions concerning the issue of meaning, and these survey results help us to gain a clear picture of people's actual responses to this issue. In particular they address the question as to whether life does have meaning at the level of popular perception.

It is abundantly clear that the suggestion that life has no meaning has very few takers at all. The British Values Survey found that only 6% of those who rarely or never attend church take such a position, while only 3% of those who attend regularly agree with them. A nihilistic approach to life is either the preserve of an intellectual elite, or it is only what we all think on a bad day!

The surveys also asked a range of other questions designed to find out more about the kind of intelligibility that people attach to life. They wanted to know if people felt that life only had meaning if a person believed in God. Similar questions were asked in relation to the issue of death and suffering or sorrow. At this point there is a very clear divergence between the views of regular church attenders and those who rarely or never attend church. As you might expect, very high percentages of those who are regular church attenders agreed with such statements. For churchgoers, the idea of God, and particularly of a personal God, is clearly and strongly connected with the idea of intelligibility. Life does have meaning, we are not here by chance, we are on earth for a purpose.

By contrast, far fewer of those who rarely or never attend church agreed with such statements. Interestingly, and probably not coincidentally, the same number of non-churchgoers who make the connection between life's intelligibility in relation to God, also believe in God as a personal being. In other words, those who aren't church attenders but who share with Christians the idea of a personal God, are very likely to extend that belief towards an explanation of the world. For this group of non-churchgoers as well as for churchgoers, life has meaning and its meaning is informed by a broadly Christian view of what that meaning might be.

The content of meaning

If the existence of God does not provide any source of meaning for those who rarely or occasionally attend church, what is the real content of any statement that life has meaning? Both the European Values Survey and the British Values Survey reveal that very high percentages of non-churchgoers, often in excess of 90%, agree with the statement that 'The meaning of life is that you try to get the best out of it'. Such a statement seems to carry a high degree of resonance at a popular level of perception in our culture.

But how should we understand such a statement? Is it simply a lowest common denominator statement which is so devoid of content that anyone could agree with it without having to think too hard about what it actually means? We do not need to be quite so pessimistic. Two factors help us to have more insight into the meaning of this phrase.

1. The importance of family. The British Values Survey asks a number of other questions which give us more information about the content of what the 'best' that we can get out of life might be. Three aspects of life emerge strongly as areas which are highly valued. They are family, friends/acquaintances, and leisure. There is a strong correlation between all three of these areas, since presumably a good deal of leisure activity will be spent in the company of family and friends. It is these areas of life that give meaning to life.

Of the three areas that we have identified, by far the most important is that of family. Amongst those who are not churchgoers, the family is listed as very important by 86% of respondents, as compared with the next most frequent category of friends, which is regarded as very important by 41% of the sample. While work is regarded as very important by a fairly high number of people, it is clear that its importance amongst non-churchgoers has much more to do with factors such as pay than to status-related issues, or to the value of a job in society. In other words, the statement that work is important is not related to any feelings about the meaning of life. Work has only a broadly utilitarian value.

Meaning, for non-churchgoers, seems to relate strongly to one's place as someone who is known and valued within a relatively small circle of people rather than to society more widely. This finding raises a number of questions about the content of the meaning of life if the family should fail for some reason.

2. The absence of transcendence. The British Values Survey asked a number of questions that have to do with issues of transcendence. These questions relate to the meaning of life and the

the issue of death. The simple fact is that a significant number of people simply never, or hardly ever, think about the meaning of life. There seems to be a considerable difference between churchgoers and non-churchgoers in this area. According to the British Values Survey, on a scale of 1 to 4, where 4 means often and 1 means never, churchgoers scored 3.36 when asked how often they think about the meaning of life, whereas non-churchgoers scored 2.76. Very similar responses were received to questions about death. In other words, although non-churchgoers agree that life does have meaning, they rarely think about what that meaning might be.

What do we make of such a finding? It would seem that for non-churchgoers, the only meaning that life might have derives not from any source beyond this world, but only from the very immediate presence of family or friends. The meaning of life is not thought through so much as experienced and that experience points to the place of close relationships as vital. These findings seem to be confirmed by the work that Roger Edrington conducted amongst his group of working class men. The absence of any immediate transcendent meaning further reinforces the importance of the family.

The family as a source of meaning

The transition from an agricultural society to an industrial and more recently to a post-industrial, information-based society, has been accompanied by great changes in family life. The structure of the family as a complex web of relationships encompassing several generations and including aunts, uncles and cousins in a system which might almost be described as a clan or tribe, has narrowed considerably as society has changed. The more mobile and much smaller nuclear family is closer to what most people in the West now understand as the family. Even within this structure, the last thirty years have witnessed a number of changes in our understanding of the family.

First of all, the family does not always mean a mother and a father and their immediate offspring. Single parenting has become much more common. The incidence of divorce and remarriage introduces the possibility that the children in a household may not be the natural children of the adults in that household. Some have advocated the idea that a homosexual or lesbian couple should be able to adopt children. Still other adults may be the father or mother of children in more than one family unit, responsible for their financial security.

Secondly, the increase in longevity means that the length of time when couples live without children in the household has increased considerably. At the same time, there seems to be more couples who make a conscious choice not to have children. The pattern of caring for older people, whether parents or not, has changed. The assumption that children will care for ageing parents in the final years of life, so important in non-Western cultures, is no longer so prevalent in the West.

Thirdly, although the practise of monogamy is still the expressed ideal within marriage, the practise of serial monogamy rather than one of non-stop, permanent monogamy is far more common than it once was. This increased likelihood of having more than one married partner in a lifetime further complicates the pattern of family life.

Fourth, the trend towards both partners in a marriage working outside of the home changes the expectations of roles within the family. It can no longer be assumed that women will take the exclusive, or even the primary responsibility for the care of children within the family. A variety of other arrangements for childcare are much more common than they were.

These are by no means the only changes affecting the family, but they certainly add up to far-reaching change of a kind which places increased pressures on traditional notions of what family life really means. The extent of many of these changes was experienced on a smaller scale in the years immediately following the post-war period and led to many predictions of the end of the family. The decades since then have demonstrated the amazing ability of the family to adapt to change. Moreover there seems to be no lessening in the desire that people express to experience family life, even if the reality does not match the hope. The European Values Survey reports that 80% of Europeans disagree with the suggestion that marriage is an outdated institution. This figure represents an increase over the number who gave such an answer in 1981.

There seems to be something of a tension in these findings. On the one hand the incidence of divorce is rising. Marriage and the family seem to be under greater pressure than ever, and yet the popularity of marriage and of the family as an institution seems to be rising according to every available measure. This tension is further heightened when one looks in more detail at expressed values within marriage and the family. On the one hand 90% of people view faithfulness as the most important quality in marriage, and yet fully 30% of married respondents take the view that sexual freedom without restraint is valid, while 50% of single people take the same view. Only 50% of the total sample think that extra-marital affairs are never justified.

How can one reconcile the popularity of marriage and family with rising divorce rates which undermine family life to such a degree? Even more problematic, how does the view that the family should be the guardian of traditional values and the greatest single source of moral teaching equate with a situation in which the family is undergoing such rapid and far-reaching change? It may well be that these contradictions actually contribute to the strain which family life is experiencing.

The weakening of other social institutions such as the erosion of a sense of community, the decline of the church, increased scepticism concerning the role of patriotism and civic duty, may well leave the family as the only point at which people experience a strong sense of belonging. In such a situation, it is perhaps not surprising that the family is seen as the primary place in which the meaning of life is expressed. But the question remains as to how realistic such expectations really are. By placing such a heavy burden on the family, it may well be that the family will finally collapse under the weight of unrealistic expectations.

If anything, those who are churchgoers have even higher expectations of family life. But at least in the case of churchgoers, the demands of family life are more often balanced by other significant relationships. For example, churchgoers are far more likely than non-churchgoers to be involved in voluntary work in the community. By receiving some meaning and sense of reward from such involvement, the practical expectations placed on the family may well be lessened. Moreover, it is possible that the churches, which reinforce the value of family life, may act as an external resource which help married partners and their families to meet the challenges of the family. A strong church forms a wider family both for those who are married and also for single people. By seeing meaning as related to a belief in God, rather than as centred entirely in family life, the family is given meaning and place in a broader framework of reference, rather than having to act as the sole source from which meaning is derived.

The Christian tradition sees marriage as containing a sacramental dimension. The reason for this perspective is that marriage and the family are seen as places which point to the sacred in human life. The human mother and father represent aspects of the care of God. The process of procreation is itself a reflection of the creative nature of God. Children are gifts from God. Their childlike qualities are understood as pointing to an aspect of the relationship between the Creator and all of his creatures. In terms of the meaning of life there is a clear difference between a view of marriage and family which has a sacred dimension, with all of the mystery that such a perspective implies, and a view which sees marriage and family as essentially functional in character. The very fact that the area of family life is seen as a place in which the meaning of life is expressed, raises the question about the place of the sacred in the framework of life's meaning.

Despoiling the sacred

A recent survey conducted amongst school children in the UK on the subject of worship in schools uncovered some remarkable material.[3] The process of conducting the research made a profound impact on the researcher himself. The formal results of the research revealed that schoolchildren had a very high opinion of the potential value of the school assembly as an opportunity for worship. Very few wished to see it discontinued, even though the quality of much of the worship left a good deal to be desired. One headmaster apparently described much of what he saw as 'Hymn, prayer, and rollicking'. Certainly the constant emphasis on good behaviour and adherence to school rules detracted somewhat from much sense of the transcendent. However, apart from the useful formal findings, the questions raised by many individual students caused the researcher to feel that the schoolchildren were being profoundly failed by the inability of anyone to address the questions of transcendence which were being raised.

What kind of questions were raised? It was clear that many pupils were pointing to some very profound religious issues. Who am I? How do people die? What does the future hold? Why do people suffer? Why is it that God doesn't seem to answer my prayers? Just as important as the questions themselves was the impression that the staff were not sure how to react to such questions. It was not that they were unable to come up with snap answers to the questions of their pupils, (who could answer such questions easily?), it was much more that they were not sure what to do with these questions at all. Should they even begin to answer questions such as these? What was the role of the school? How could they speak to issues that they had never answered or perhaps never seriously considered themselves? If one did give time to such questions, what would be an appropriate response? The impression of the researcher was that on the whole these essentially religious questions were simply not answered, either by the assemblies, or by individual contact with the pupils.

Does it really matter whether such questions are dealt with? The survey revealed that only between 10-12% of the pupils had any contact with any religious organisation at all, so in the majority of cases it was not possible for these questions to be asked in such a context. What about the family: isn't that the best place to deal with such matters? Possibly so, but here lies part of the problem. Many of the questions were themselves a reflection of the failure of some aspects of family life. For example, one child commented, 'I used to believe in God, but then my parents got divorced.' The one place where the sacred aspects of life could be experienced had been despoiled. If the sacred has been removed, where can such questions be asked? The impression was given by many pupils that the lack of any place in which profound questions could be safely raised had meant that the questions simply stopped. The questions had not been resolved, but the part of their being that raised such matters had gradually shrivelled and died. Deep longings were buried and this at an age when profound decisions about aspects of transcendence were being made.

If the question of life's meaning is intimately connected with morality, how then can we speak about a basis for morality? An essentially secular worldview suggests that the meaning of life is to get the best out of life. But if the place where that best is sought for has already been despoiled by the failure of significant relationships, where does one turn?

The issues of fear and loss raised so poignantly by the schoolchildren in the survey are ultimately questions that are traditionally addressed by religion. Here lies the central dilemma for the unbeliever. The impulse to seemingly break free from religion and to attempt to find meaning elsewhere seems doomed to defeat. All too often it leads, not to a framework of meaning without belief, so much as to different belief. Reason or science or both have often taken the place of the old god, but such elevation tends to remain empty because it confuses the quest for explanation with the search for meaning. The consequence of such confusion is the creation of yet more paradoxes. It is estimated that in one of the European cities with the lowest attendance at public Christian worship, Paris, some 450,000 people regularly consult registered fortune tellers.[4] The city of Voltaire has become the city of those who search for hidden meaning amidst the uncertainty of the movements of the planets.

The emerging problem of the Western world
It is not one of unbelief so much as the direction in which belief is pointed.

It is not one of morality so much as the basis for morality.

It is not the conclusion that life has no meaning, it is more that the search for meaning is anchored in institutions that may break apart under the strain of being asked to deliver that which they were never intended to produce.

It is not that the sacred is not sought so much that few dare to speak about it.

Christians can hardly claim to have been lonely prophets speaking words of truth which have been ignored. The failings of the church have also been part of the problem. But the very distance and apparent irrelevance of the church have curiously given rise to a new opportunity. The very failure of the church has caused it to consider afresh the content of its message. It is just possible that a church which is able to recover its sense of mission may be able to speak about the problem of belief and faith. It cannot do so with a triumphant voice, but with an attitude of repentance and humility. It must share the pain of those to whom it seeks to speak. The church must not come with the sword of judgement or with any other weapon of domination. It must come instead with a basin of water and a simple towel to address the tears of a culture in crisis.

CHAPTER EIGHT

THE EXHAUSTION OF THE WEST

The phrase, 'the exhaustion of the West' is one that has been coined by Alexander Solzhenitsyn to describe the present dilemma of the West.[1] It is a phrase that also carries a high degree of resonance for those who have looked thoughtfully at the Western church. When we consider matters as complex as the culture of a society or the life of a religion, it is all too easy to confuse activity with life and energy with power. No doubt there are many who would look at some aspects of the life of the West, especially in the United States, and wonder what Solzhenitsyn is talking about. Many businessmen who visit the United States from Europe are impressed by the vibrancy of the business community that they find there. It is possible to visit and live in many parts of the West and conclude that Solzhenitsyn is simply a Russian who has never come to terms with society in the West.

In much the same way, a Christian could move from lively church to lively church in a variety of Western countries and conclude that there is a great deal of life in the church – nowhere more so than in the United States. To the European observer, American Christianity seems to be in the prime of its life. But such a conclusion misses the main point. Christianity may be able to command the allegiance of many who still attend worship services, but it no longer acts as a wellspring for our culture. This is true whether we are speaking about the United States, where significant numbers of people still attend church, or the United Kingdom (where more people attend church on a Sunday than attend soccer matches on a Saturday), or any other Western land. The church is a minority concern in every Western country apart from the United

States and even in that land there is real cause for concern. The situation in the United States feels to many observers rather like that which prevailed in Britain at the end of the nineteenth century. At that time the churches faced the new century with great confidence. They had great energy, were noted for the number of new and imaginative evangelistic initiatives that abounded, commanded considerable political influence, were socially active and generally wealthy. But few had noticed that the church was no longer influencing the development of the culture. It was this failure above all others that was to prove devastating for the church in Britain and elsewhere.

The contrast of the fortunes of the church in the West at the end of the twentieth century with that at the beginning of the same century is astonishing. At the beginning of the century the church in every Western country looked confidently at both the home and overseas mission fields.[2] The previous century had seen unprecedented advances for the Christian faith around the world, and although it was recognised that the working classes in some countries were somewhat ambivalent and occasionally hostile to the church, the security of the church amongst the dominant middle classes helped them to feel that this situation could be corrected. It was also known that some of those in the intellectual and cultural elite were strongly opposed to Christianity, but they were a very small minority and some of their activities, for example the establishment of atheist chapels, were little short of ridiculous.

So confident were the majority in the churches that few, if any, foresaw the extent of a decline which has been cataclysmic for the church in the West as a whole. The irony of the situation is clearly seen when we remember that at the end of a century when the church in Western Europe has been entirely free to propagate the faith, and the church in Eastern Europe has been severely restrained from doing so, there are now more worshippers in Moscow than in London.[3] The revolution in the former East Germany which brought down the Berlin wall began in the churches of that land. It is hard to imagine the church in any Western European nation having a similar social and political impact.

It is a situation which is all the more surprising when seen in the context of the worldwide church. The twentieth century has seen the spread of the Christian faith around the world to such an extent that for the first time since the church began, Christianity can now be properly described as a world faith and not just as a European or Western faith. The confidence and vibrancy of the church in Latin America, Africa and many parts of Asia stands in stark contrast with the apologetic, subdued and almost defeated seige mentality that emanates from much of the church in the West.

This striking contrast is reinforced by the fact that many Christians in the West are hopelessly ill-informed about the situation of the church around the world. All too often the pessimism engendered by a story of constant decline at home is projected onto the rest of the church. To be fair, this phenomenon is not confined to Christians. There are many outside the church who simply know nothing of the amazing impact that the church is making in many societies around the world. When the Polish shipyard workers in Gadansk began their action which led to the formation of Solidarity, the greatest surprise in the secular press was not that shipyard workers were resisting the authorities. It was instead the sight of thousands of working men, in their workclothes, on their knees in front of the shipyard, receiving communion. These men knew about Marx but preferred St. Peter and St. Paul. Such an idea was almost incomprehensible to the secular Western mind at that time.

But, to return to our theme, it was not that no one at the beginning of the century saw the danger that the church was in. There were some notable prophetic voices, not the least of whom was an Archbishop of Canterbury, William Temple. But either these lonely prophets were not understood, or there was simply not the inclination or capacity to change. (One hears the same prophetic voices speaking in America today and wonders if they too are being ignored[4]). Faced with the dramatic loss of numbers and influence in society, an all too common feeling amongst church leaders has been one of bewilderment accompanied by the hope that something, anything, will somehow turn up to change matters. This Micawber-like attitude has not been rewarded.

Responses to decline

Not all have stood idly by. Indeed, all across the Western world, there have been those church leaders who have given much in order to help the church through its time of difficulty. How then has the church reacted to the threatening storm clouds of the twentieth century?

1. The call to return. The seriousness of the potential decline facing the church was not easy to detect in the early part of the century. In England, the message was rather a mixed one. Many denominations did not peak in their actual membership figures until 1930, even though attendances had fallen in some denominations. It was all too easy to view the social turmoil of the inter-war years as the main problem that the churches faced. Following the end of the Second World War many church leaders began to think in terms of rebuilding the life of the churches as if the first half of the century had been only a temporary blip in the earlier progress of the church. Indeed, in some European countries, and more noticeably in the United States, the early years of the 1950s did indeed witness some growth in church attendances and even membership. This growth was such that it left the churches entirely unprepared for the dramatic losses in attendance and membership that began at the end of the 1950s and accelerated in the 1960s.

The nature of this pattern caused some church leaders to think in terms of the various populations of the West coming back to the church, rather than to look at how the church might need to change. In this sense the problem was seen as being 'out there' rather than 'at home'. This tendency was encouraged by the strongly pastoral perspective of many leaders. The church in the West had always seen patterns of ebb and flow throughout the centuries, but the essentially Christian character of the culture of the West had never been seriously called into question, with the possible exception of the eighteenth century in certain European countries. For more than a thousand years, the orientation of the church in the West had been towards the pastoral and teaching task of drawing lost sheep back to the fold and of teaching the faithful how to live the Christian life. Mission had never been seen as something that took place in the

West but, if it happened at all, occurred only in distant and scarcely-known lands. The potential absurdity of calling back to the church those who had never yet been was not really appreciated.

It was not that there weren't some notable converts. In England, some who had been avowedly atheistic in their youth, Malcolm Muggeridge, Lord Hailsham and Philip Toynbee, to name a few, discovered faith in a moving and sometimes high profile fashion.[5] However, it was legitimate to think in terms of these men returning to something that they had known, even if they had rejected and pilloried the church throughout a good deal of their lives. But there were increasingly many in Europe whose connection with the church was sufficiently tenuous that the idea of calling them to return to the church was plainly absurd.

2. *The call to relevance.*   Some church leaders saw the flaws in simply calling on people to return to an unchanged and unchanging church. Their call was directed towards the church. If the population of the West was ever to take the church seriously, then the church needed to change in ways that would clearly demonstrate the relevance of the church to the modern world. For these leaders, the task of the church needed to be redefined. Mission, evangelism, sacrament, salvation and miracle: all these and much more needed to be understood in new and relevant ways. The age of dialogue had begun – dialogue with Marxists, with those of other faiths, with secular humanists, with science and with philosophy. We began to hear of the need for a secular faith, of liberation theology, of demythologising the Bible, of social action and a political agenda.

But the newly, apparently relevant faith did not seem to win many converts except amongst those who were already Christians. Indeed the outcome of such a process has all too tragically led many to the conclusion that they no longer believed, and confirmed the suspicions of those outside the church that they were right never to have believed at all. There is perhaps no more tragic a sight than the priest and theologian who has lost his faith. In many cases, such individuals have gone on teaching theology to those who do believe, but the gap of communication has become singular and deep. In recent years, there are many who have pointed to such developments as representing little more than the effective secularisation of the church. It was not that the church was preparing to speak to a secular society, it was more that secular society was evangelising the church.

3. The call to unity. The painful legacy of the division of Christianity, which produced worldwide conflicts and intolerance amongst Christians in the aftermath of the Reformation, did not end with the various settlements following the years of religious war in Europe. Although for the most part Christians have not fought each other with physical weapons since the middle of the 17th century, the war of words has continued since that time. The ecumenical movement, which traces its origins to the Edinburgh Missionary Conference of 1910, called for new understandings, for peace and for reconciliation. The gradual rapprochement of the major Christian denominations in the West has proceeded apace during much of the twentieth century.

The conviction of many was that the Christian church would simply not have a credible message while divisions amongst Christians were so obvious. Certainly the popular perception that all wars and conflict are caused by religion, was powerfully shaped by the conflicts surrounding the post-Reformation era. (Although quite how the European wars of the twentieth century were caused by religion is rarely explained.) Moreover, there is much anecdotal evidence that even apart from the actual physical conflict of Christians, the sheer multiplicity of churches, sects and cults has been confusing for those outside of the church. One has sometimes heard the objection, 'How can I know which church is right when there are so many of them?' However, my own experience of ministry in inner city Birmingham did not reveal much anxiety on this point on the part of those who had never met a Christian before. I more often met those who thought that all churches were equally wrong than I found those anxiously struggling to find the right church!

The hope that a united church would have a much more credible, and therefore effective, witness than many separate churches does not seem to have been borne out by much evidence from around the Western world. However, this does not mean that the ecumenical movement has produced no fruit at all. The climate of co-operation and partnership has developed enormously in the latter part of the twentieth century. True, the momentum towards developing single, national churches has largely faded, but actual on-the-ground understanding amongst Christians has developed to such an extent that denominational affiliation is now very low on the priority list for most Christians when deciding which local church to join. But this new unity tends to describe almost the only achievement of the ecumenical movement. Its impact has been largely amongst Christians. The evidence that the call to unity has by itself impacted the world outside is scant indeed.

4. The call to renewal.   A radically different view of relevance, and indeed of unity, has emerged during the twentieth century from that stream of the church which is sometimes called the Pentecostal and Charismatic renewal. The early Pentecostal denominations saw themselves as 'revival outside of the church'. More recently their self-understanding has been to see themselves as a grouping of denominations linked by a common experience of the 'baptism of the Holy Spirit'. The Charismatic renewal, which emerged in the late 1950s, is characterised by the same experience of 'baptism in the Spirit', but the members of this renewal have not left their churches to join one or other of the Pentecostal denominations.[6] They have instead mostly stayed within their respective churches with the vision of renewing or reviving the traditional denominations. In this sense they see themselves as the forerunners of revival within the church. More recently, a third stream, the House Church or New Church movement, has developed alongside both the Charismatic and Pentecostal movements.[7]

A dominant theme within renewal groups has been to emphasise the work of the Holy Spirit in bringing life and vitality to the church in such a way that those outside of the churches would be dramatically impacted. An emphasis on healing, on the supernatural and even on exorcism was all seen as part of a restoration of New Testament Christianity. The emphasis has been on 'apostolic success' rather than 'apostolic succession'.

The growth of this call to renewal has been dramatic. Some

estimate that somewhere between 500,000 and 1,000,000 Christians in Britain, and far more in some other Western countries, belong to one or other of the churches in this grouping. In some countries in Europe, Pentecostals are the largest Protestant group. But some argue that the call to renewal operates only on the margins of most Western societies. Certainly the view of those in the charismatic churches that their lively worship would attract large numbers of the unchurched has turned out to be largely unfounded. Where growth has taken place, it is likely that factors other than lively charismatic worship have been important catalysts for many (though not all) of those who have joined.

A missionary church

The categories described above are by no means exhaustive nor are they compartmentalised. There are those who would fit easily into two or more of these groups. However, taken together, these movements represent the primary response of the Christian community to the radical separation that has taken place between the Christian faith and twentieth-century Western culture. But more recently there has come a realisation that it is no longer effective merely to assist the church to become more efficient at acting out what already is. It is necessary for the church to rethink its stance entirely and to become a missionary church within the West. It is not likely that the peoples of the West are going to return to the church of their own volition; it will be necessary for the church to go to them.

However, a relevance that goes so far that it actually abandons the core message of the church, hardly advances the cause of the church. The local unity of the church may, on occasion, make it more effective, but it does not by itself represent a missionary strategy. A more lively style of worship may be attractive to some, but it is simply a puzzle to others and a puzzle which needs to be explained.

The idea that the West in general and Europe in particular is a mission field, is one which has gradually gained currency since the observation of the French worker-priests that France could best be described as a largely pagan country.[8] But what does such a term really mean? There is every danger that the description of the West as a mission field might simply become a truism with no real content. In what way is a missionary church any different to the church which has existed for so long in the West? Five areas are critically important in such a situation.

Strategy for Mission

The often unstated strategy of many churches in the West has been one which has centred on evangelising the natural fringe of the church. Every church has natural pastoral contacts which arise from the ongoing life of the church. There are those who attend the various organisations attached to the church. These may be the familiar Sunday Schools, mother and toddler groups, men's groups, youth groups, and uniformed organisations. In addition to the formal structures of church life, the usual contact that comes from baptisms, weddings, funerals and counselling services add a considerable number of potential relationships from which new worshippers and members are often drawn. Conventional wisdom suggests that a growing church is one which is effective in evangelising its fringe and in expanding the number of fringe contacts. Churches which are growing even more rapidly are often skilled at evangelising the fringes of other churches in addition to their own!

But in a mission situation this strategy has its flaws. As we have noted in earlier chapters, there is growing evidence that a significant gap has emerged between the commited core of worshippers and those who are outside of the life of the church. In other words, the fringe membership of most churches in the West is shrinking as well as the committed membership, and the opportunity to expand the fringe is becoming much more difficult. In many countries, even if every church were completely successful in evangelising everyone who is part of this natural fringe, the church would still only have succeeded in touching the lives of a minority of people. The large majority of society lies well outside of the fringe of church life.

The strategy of evangelising the fringe can be characterised as 'ingrab' more than 'outreach'. It is essentially a strategy which emphasises a 'come to us' approach to mission.[9] Communicating with the majority beyond the fringe requires strategies which allow the interaction of the church with communities of people well away from the familiar territory of the local church.

Ministry beyond ministers

The primary approach to ministry in the Western church has been to concentrate on the pastoral and teaching ministries. Many ministers describe themselves as 'pastor-teachers'. The New Testament describes ministry as encompassing three other important areas. The ministries of the apostle, the prophet and the evangelist stand together with those of the pastor and the teacher in order to constitute a missionary church.[10] What do these terms mean? The New Testament records the names of apostles other than those of the original twelve. The wider use of this term means 'one who establishes the church'. In this sense, an apostle is one who is the church before the church comes into being. Their very person guarantees the nature of the church until the work of mission brings the whole community of the church into a living reality. Apostles begin new work. In a church which goes out to people rather than waits for them to come, there is a need for those who will be apostles to whole segments of society which are presently outside of the community of the church.

The prophet in the New Testament was important in giving inspired and creative direction to the task of mission. Waiting to hear the voice of God for a given situation gave insight as to what the Spirit of God was doing outside of the life of the church. The task of mission is not to do God's job for him, but to co-operate with that which he is already doing. The prophet would hear and offer direction for effective mission to take place.

The evangelist in the New Testament was able to interpret the message of the gospel in ways which were appropriate for the culture of those who were interacting with that message. The essential meaning of the gospel needed forms very unlike those of its original Jewish context if those who were unfamiliar with the world of the synagogue were ever to receive the message. The subcultures of existing churches can form insurmountable obstacles for those who stand well outside of those structures. It is all too easy to confuse the form in which the gospel is encased with the message itself. It is more likely to be the form than the content of the message which is rejected by those who are beyond the fringe of church life.

What happens to those with the gifts of apostle, prophet and evangelist in a church which is centred so strongly on the ministry gifts of the pastor and the teacher? It is rather likely that there is no natural opening for such people in a church which does not have a missionary structure. In the recent past, those who had these gifts were sent abroad as missionaries, or they gravitated towards what we might call para-church agencies working to stimulate the church towards specialist concerns. In the Catholic church the many communities of the religious, the monastic orders, were able to absorb such giftings. In the emerging missionary church of the West these apostolic gifts will be needed in the main body of the church.

The laity in mission

A missionary church cannot rely on the professional ministry for the primary work of mission. The role of the laity is critical because it is the lay members of the church who have the greatest contact with those who are outside of the normal structures of church life. In such a situation the task of clergy is not so much to engage in mission themselves, as to support the laity in their mission. This is a radically different situation from that which pertains when the majority of society considers itself to be Christian. The task of the clergy in a situation where the church is almost indistinguishable from society as a whole, is seen as related almost entirely to the traditional role of priest as carer. The task of the laity is therefore to support the priest in his role.

However, in the critical transitional stage, as society distances itself from the church whilst the church still fulfills its traditional pastoral role, the laity feels ill-equipped to deal with the task of mission. The result is that the clergy are expected to be the agents of mission. But this is a hopelessly unrealistic expectation. The gifts of God are not given exclusively to the clergy but to the whole church. Mission can only take place when the implications of this reality are fully reflected in the life of the church. The role of the laity as the primary agents of mission requires that they be both committed to the community of the church and yet also free to engage in that mission. Unfortunately, a church which is not yet structured for mission requires those who are committed to the Christian community to use their time to support the internal structures of the church. There is therefore an unbearable tension. Fully-devoted members of the laity are expected to maintain the structures of the church, give full attention to their family, and also engage in mission. A truly missionary church will need to structure its life in such a way that the laity are free to discover their missionary vocation.

Training in Mission

The content and style of training for clergy engaged in mission, rather than the traditional functions of pastoring and teaching, will be significantly different. But the critical issue for a missionary church will not be just the training of clergy, but the training of the laity. Two aspects of this training are important. First the issue of discipleship. The church of the first few centuries laid a great emphasis on the teaching of new converts (the catechumenate). So important was the preparation of new converts that the process could easily sometimes take two years. Even then, candidates for baptism would normally be interviewed by the Bishop to ensure that they were ready to be baptised. Often the baptisms would be performed at Easter. The church marked the event of preparation by fasting for forty days before Easter, (the origin of Lent). But in a situation where everyone in society was a Christian the ingredient of instruction became much less important. The norms of a society which lived and breathed Christian values were sufficient and effective as a means of teaching. But the emergence of a post-Christian society introduces a degree of confusion. In such a situation the tradition of training in discipleship is no longer present and the introduction of such a rigorous discipline is both difficult and yet vital. A missionary church will emphasise the need to be a disciple and not simply a believer.

Secondly, the training of disciples to be missionaries needs to continue beyond the period of preparation for baptism or confirmation. The most critical aspect of training is in the area of what the church calls apologetics. In the face of a hostile culture, the Christian lay missionary needs to be able to give an intelligent account of the faith that they profess. It is not that many are ever argued into faith, but a predominantly non-Christian culture will not give any hearing to those who cannot give some intelligent account of what they believe. Apologetics are important in clearing away unthinking objections so that the Christian message can be be given a proper hearing.

A missiology for the West

Those who are in training to serve the church, whether as professional clergy or as lay people, are exposed to a wide range of disciplines. They learn some theology, ecclesiology, church history and doctrine. They may even learn some practical ministry skills. They almost certainly do not learn missiology.

The study of missions has been a relatively new discipline for the church. A great deal of mission study revolves around the issue of culture. How does one communicate the gospel across significant cultural boundaries? Partly because the West has only recently been viewed as a mission field and partly because we all too easily assume that we already understand the culture in which we live, mission studies for the West hardly exist. In reality, the problems of communication, language and culture are just as significant in the context of the West. Not only is there the issue of the direction of the mainstream of Western culture, but there are many hundreds of sub-cultures within that mainstream, some of which are both difficult to understand and which seem to be highly resistant to the gospel. Not the least of these is the sub-culture of youth.[11] Church life itself often represents a sub-culture which introduces barriers of understanding between those in the church and those who have had little if any contact with the church. A missionary church needs a good missiology.

The false god of method in mission

The concern to help the church become a missionary church can all too easily be confused with the notion that what is important is only the application of a good methodology. The church in the West, under pressure to be more effective in its life and witness, has been too easily beguiled by an interest in methods and techniques. Nowhere has this been more evidenced than in that aspect of mission which we call evangelism. The influence of North American evangelical Christianity has been very strong amongst evangelicals throughout the West. During the twentieth century there has emerged a strong strain of pragmatism which has tended to emphasise the importance of finding the right methods. As Andrew Walker observes of evangelicals, 'We are so obsessed with success in terms of what one critic has called the 'numbers game', that we have majored on method at the expense of theological reflection and sound doctrine.'[12] Walker goes on to note that it was the larger than life American evangelist Billy Sunday who first introduced the very pragmatic notion of 'a price for a soul' when he charged churches a set amount for the converts that he passed on to them. Billy Sunday, operating as he did at the beginning of the twentieth century and setting his evangelistic appeal in the context of theatrical showmanship, was the forerunner of much of the tele-evangelism and other larger scale crusades which have become such a part of some American evangelical Christianity.

This is not to say that good methodology does not have some place in the life and mission of the church. Certainly one is not arguing for the application of bad methods! Moreover, one can certainly observe many churches which have consistently applied one or other of the various evangelistic methods that are available and have seen some encouraging results over a period of time. But closer examination often reveals that this 'success' is most often amongst those who are on the natural fringe of church life. These are the people who understand the culture, language and basic concepts of the Christian gospel. The main focus of such methodology is not so much to communicate or explain the fundamental message of the gospel, but rather to help people who are part of the fringe to appropriate the message for themselves, to see its immediate relevance in such a way that they will make a response.

But when it comes to the question of communicating the gospel message to those who are beyond the fringe, the application of good methods alone is deeply flawed. Four key objections need to be noted. First, a number of observers have noted that an uncritical commitment to pragmatism above every other consideration has much more to do with the values of secular Western culture than with the gospel of Jesus Christ.[13] It is hardly likely that one can evangelise a culture with a gospel that stresses very different values, when one is so committed to methods which actually reinforce the values of the culture you are seeking to challenge.

Secondly, not only is the integrity of the message called into question, but there is a danger that the content is actually subtly corrupted. Research from many sources indicates that most people become Christians through personal friendship.[14] Such an observation is fine as far as it goes. Indeed, a thoughtful person would expect this to be true. Many important life decisions are informed by conversations with those whom we trust, rather than by complete strangers. Such knowledge can cause us to place even greater value on the relationships that we have. However, to reduce this information to a method or a technique is quite another matter. As William Abraham comments:

> Unless we are very careful, such delicate matters of friendship and love will be turned into one more utilitarian means or tool to increase the statistics of church membership. Before we know what is happening sacred human relationships will have lost their integrity and the distinctive character of Christian love will have been eroded by an evangelistic orientation that construes them not as ends in themselves but as means to an end.[15]

Thirdly, as I have implied earlier on in this section, a purely pragmatic appeal to methods and techniques does not always work, even on its own terms. There is no evidence to suggest that anyone has succeeded in reaching large numbers of unchurched people on the basis of a newly-discovered method alone. As far as those beyond the fringe are concerned, using methods is not the right method! Something rather more fundamental is required.

Fourthly, those who value the New Testament record, and who point to the account of the spectacular growth of the church in the

Acts of the Apostles, underline the astonishing absence of methods and techniques. The missiologist Charles Tabor says of the church of the New Testament:

> It did not establish empirical, numerical goals for its outreach. The jubilant references to numbers – 3,000, 5,000, and so on – all represent rejoicing after the fact, not projections for the future. The New Testament church did not display a preoccupation with organisation, methods, or techniques, but showed total confidence in the intrinsic power of the message itself.[16]

It is this 'confidence in the intrinsic power of the message' that helps us to glimpse what a rather more fundamental response to the unchurched might be.

The battleground of church growth

Nowhere has the debate about whether the use of methods assists or corrupts the gospel message been fiercer than that which surrounds the Church Growth movement.[17] This movement began with the work of Dr Donald M'Gavran (an American second-generation missionary in India for much of his life). His serious study of the methods that could be applied to missions began after his formal retirement and were centred at the School of World Mission in Pasadena, California. M'Gavran's work included a strong polemical edge which often illicited strong reactions from those who objected to what looked like an over concern with numbers as the sole measurement of success.

But what both the advocates and opponents of the Church Growth movement often missed was that the real heart of M'Gavran's work was not the use of methods as such. The driving force behind his work centred on the role of culture as something which formed an impenetrable barrier to the gospel. This concern for the effect of culture arose as a result of his own experiences on the mission field. M'Gavran had been only too aware of the extent to which Christianity in some parts of India was strongly identified with the culture of the West. The boundary fence of the mission compound was more than just a physical boundary. The territory inside the mission compound was actually an extension of European or American culture. Everything outside the compound was where India really began. The mission compound signified the place where West and East met. This dividing line meant that when an Indian wished to become a Christian he had to change more than just his religion. In many important respects he had to become a second class Westerner in order to become a Christian.

This barrier of culture deeply disturbed M'Gavran. He could see that this was a situation that prevailed in many missions around the world. Nor was this just a phenomenon which only affected missions outside of the West. The Western world itself is not just one uniform culture, but is composed of a whole mosaic of cultures and sub-cultures. Viewed in this way, the various sub-cultures in the West, the sub-culture of youth, of class and even of unbelief, have effectively been isolated from the gospel. The insulating effect of culture has been reinforced by the tendency of the church, whether as a whole, or whether as individual denominations, to become self-contained sub-cultures which have forgotten how to transcend the barrier of culture.

There is perhaps no clearer example of the tendency of particular denominations to create their own unique sub-culture than the late Victorian achievement of the nonconformist denominations in England. A whole culture which encompassed institutions such as the Band of Hope, the Sunday School, Mutual Improvement Classes for men, and family events known as Pleasant Sunday Afternoons were reinforced by well-known heroes: Spurgeon, Haddon, Dale and Clifford. They had their own newspapers, schools, publishing houses and even international organisations. The Liberal Party had become their special political expression. So powerful was this sub-culture, that it looked to the future of the twentieth century with a self-confidence bordering on arrogance.[18] Yet by the middle of the twentieth century the effectiveness of this sub-culture was as hopelessly lost as was the Liberal Party's hold on power. The world outside had changed, the nonconformist sub-culture had remained the same, tragically confusing the gospel message with such cultural experiences as 'signing the pledge'. It is precisely this fatal confusion of gospel with culture that should sound warning bells for American Christianity today.

The result of this cultural isolation has often been that the Christian gospel has not been rejected so much as it has never been heard. If the church in the West is ever to become a missionary church it will need to learn how to break out of its own mission compounds, to create the church afresh in the various sub-cultures of society. This is not really a matter of methods or techniques, so much as learning how to be the church in new ways. The 'intrinsic power of the message' only becomes authentically released when this process takes place.

Cross-cultural communication

The existence of a static Christian sub-culture amongst many Christian groups, where the forms in which the message comes are seen as important as the message itself, produces a situation where either potential converts are compelled to leave their culture and join the static, alien culture of the church, or they are asked to live in a permanent situation of compartmentalisation. In either case it is unlikely that any who become Christians in such a context will have a significant impact on those around them. This form of becoming a Christian causes the loss of credibility in the workplace, the family and in other social relationships. Being 'born again' is understood by those in secular culture as the process of leaving the real world and escaping to an incomprehensible world of myth and private faith. The explanation for such a move will often be that the person who has become a Christian needs the comfort and support that religion can provide. It is to opt out of life rather than to adopt a horizon that makes real sense of life.

Although the stance of the cult or the sect will be to see the prevailing culture of society as hostile, and the sub-culture of the church as a place of safety, the main Christian tradition has been to attempt to transform culture. But the attempt to transform culture has proved to be an almost impossible task for the church in the West. In part this has been because many Christians have been confused about the relationship of the Christian faith to culture. We have only recently passed from a time when to be Christian was to be Western, and to be Western was to be Christian. The idea that society in the West was a Christian society, even if everyone in the culture was not an active Christian, has only recently passed out of the consciousness of many societies in the West. This assumption has been so recent that it is by no means clear to many, whether in the church or outside of it, just what difference it makes to be a Christian. Belonging to a church is easily equated with belonging to any other interest group, rather than containing the idea that Christian faith implies a radical commitment to a new kind of society.

This confusion tends to place the Christian on the margins of society, even when the ideology to which he or she is committed is not to escape the culture, but to transform it. As the anthropologist Charles Kraft has argued, culture is primarily challenged and changed by those who are insiders rather than outsiders.[19] How can the church confront this basic dilemma? A missionary church begins with the task of cross-cultural communication. This is a very subversive activity. The initial goal is not necessarily to convert large numbers of people, so much as to convert the few who will remain insiders in the culture. It is vitally important that such believers will be both thoroughly schooled in the Christian faith and yet not drawn out of the culture into the sub-culture of the church. The intention must be to allow those who are truly insiders to create forms of the church which will allow the message of Christianity to be interpreted and lived in new cultural forms.

It is perhaps much easier to understand how this principle works by looking at cultures which are radically different from our own.[20] Very recently, in some Islamic countries, relatively large numbers of people have become followers of Jesus, but have attempted to remain within Islamic society rather than leave their culture to become part of an alien church culture. The concept has been that of creating the Jesus mosque. In principle this has been no different from the recent creation of many Jewish Christian groups who now worship Jesus as the Messiah and have formed Messianic synagogues. These highly creative and controversial developments have echoed a much earlier movement of the Christian faith from its original Jewish context to the Hellenistic world of the Greek believers. The first gentile churches of the early church must have seemed just as controversial to the original Christians, many of whom still worshipped in synagogues.

How can this be interpreted in a Western context? Some radical expressions of new forms of the church have already been born amongst young people. The strategy of creating youth churches which use forms which many adults would find very alien indeed, has resulted in significant numbers of young people hearing the Christian gospel for the very first time. Forms of the church which will communicate much more effectively with adults who stand totally outside of the church are currently being dreamt of and experimented with. It is still too early to say how many of these initiatives will turn out to be valid expressions of the Christian message. What is certain is that creative experimentation is essential if the task of cross-cultural communication is to proceed.

Those who are sent as conventional missionaries from the West to other lands spend many years in training. It is considered essential for missionaries to learn as much about the culture to which they are sent as possible. But those who are trained to be leaders in the Western church do not learn much about the culture of those who are outside of the church. Is that because our training institutions make the assumption that those who have been born in the West will already understand the culture in which they were brought up? It may be that they do, but I remain to be convinced. My own experience of ministerial training is that clergy are actually trained to understand the culture of the church, but not to reflect very much on the culture of those outside of the church. It is as if such information would be a waste of time. Such an attitude is understandable in a church which sees its function as meeting the needs of the faithful. But if the church is to be a missionary church, it is essential that the culture of the unchurched is grappled with. The church may need new teachers to assist such a process to take place.

In addition to studying the culture of the people to whom they will go, missionaries are also required to learn the language of those same people. In one sense the task of learning a new language never ends. It is becoming increasingly clear that the language of belief and the language of unbelief are very different. A new missionary church in the West will need to learn this new language of unbelief. In learning to communicate it will be important for the church to recognise the points of contact between the Christian message and a world for whom that message is unfamiliar and very foreign. At the heart of the Christian gospel lies a message of hope. One of the features of the exhausted West is the absence of hope. It is an absence which is so profound that any talk of hope seems foolish and empty. Methodology and techniques by themselves do not produce a human point of contact for such communication to take place. But identifying the places where hope might break through in the culture of the West is part of the missionary task.

CHAPTER NINE

EXPERIENCING THE TRANSCENDENCE OF GOD

Despite all that has happened in the modern world: the charge of Feuerbach, Marx and others that all religion is simply a creation of man; the work of Laplace who saw no need for God in order to explain the world; the proclamation of Nietzsche that God is dead; despite all this, we have seen that belief in God remains puzzlingly widespread. Yet to speak about God is not easy. As Pannenberg observes: 'Anyone who tries to speak of God today can no longer count on being immediately understood'.[1] There is a sense in which a kind of practical atheism forms the framework in which Western man, including Christians, live today. Talk of God needs careful explanation.

Yet the question of God remains, even for those who find belief in God difficult and occasionally impossible. The question arises simply because man exists. In one sense, man does not ask the question about God, man's very existence raises the question of God.[2] It seems as if man has an insatiable curiosity about the world and his place in it. Anthropology speaks of this phenomenon as man's openness to the world and maintains that this particular characteristic marks man out as different from the animals.[3] Man's questioning is driven by a desire to transcend his situation, to continually press beyond his own world into the world of the unknown. Not that man always receives answers. Camus has spoken of the 'hopeless gap between the question of man and the silence of the universe'.[4]

How then can we begin to speak about God in the midst of this silent universe? The religious tradition of the West has always spoken about the transcendence and the immanence of God. The transcendence of God is that aspect of God which is other than the created order. God is beyond that which he has created; he existed before time began and will be present at the end of time. The transcendence of God anchors meaning and morals in an objectivity that is not subject to change. The grandeur of transcendence does not imply remoteness, but it does suggest otherness. The Creator can never be entirely the same as that which is created.

Immanence is that aspect of God which is expressed in the created order itself. God is not just over and above the creation, he is also powerfully in it. The problem for modern man is not the question of immanence. It is relatively easy to look at the created order and experience something of God, even if that something is no more than God as a life-force. The problem has been to experience something of God as transcendent.[5] Strangely, the loss of the notion of transcendence has often lead to a loss of the more immediate experience of immanence. The erosion of a sense that the universe has meaning seems to bring a despair which leads to the loss of wonder and mystery in the transcendence of God which are so often the hallmarks of experiencing the immanence of God.

False transcendence

The reaction to modernism described in Chapter Three as the 'new religious impulse' attempts to talk about some aspects of transcendence. For example, the appropriation by much New Age thinking of many Eastern religious ideas contains a very specific appeal to an aspect of transcendence. The very phrase, Transcendental Meditation, has become instantly recognisable throughout the West as part of the new experimentation in alternative religious traditions. But what is really meant by such talk of transcendence?

The writer Michael Fuss has produced a very detailed overview and analysis of New Age origins and thinking.[6] His work confirms the view of Mangalwadi, referred to in Chapter One, that New Age thinking is not just Hinduism come West, so much as a reinterpretation of many Eastern ideas in a Western context and tradition. Fuss traces the early origins of this pattern of thought from Swedenborg (1688–1772) and then shows how important was the impact of the romantic idealism of the nineteenth century, particularly in Germany. The ideas of gnosticism, an old opponent of Christianity, have strongly influenced this movement and has helped to define what is really intended by the notion of transcendence.

The point about this kind of transcendence is that it is really a disguised immanence, albeit immanence of a radical kind. Fuss calls it an experience of 'transcendence within immanence', the 'immanence beyond.'[7] The appeal is not to the kind of transcendence which springs from a revelation of a truly transcendent God who comes from beyond the cosmos, but rather an experience of a very primitive encounter with the cosmos itself. It speaks of the 'dark profundity of the cosmos whence higher forces originate and exercise their influence on humanity.'[8]

Visser 't Hooft makes the same point. He notes the influence of Schopenhauer who brought the traditions of theosophy, anthroposophy and Eastern spirituality to the West. He says: 'Its attraction is not only its exotic quality. It is what the neo-pagans had been looking for, 'religion without revelation' in which the distinctions between God, man and nature tend to disappear.'[9] This kind of experience of God is one in which the forces of the created world, whether as an encounter with the forces of nature, or of human sexuality, or of formerly unexplored human potential, or the powers of the occult, are seen as a heightened immanence which gives the illusion of transcendence. In many ways this is religion at its most primitive, offering escape from the material world, or power over that same world. It does not offer any real account of the meaning of life so much as providing ways of avoiding such questions, and as such is really a false transcendence.

Transcendence in the traditional world of religion

The various experiences offered by what I have called 'false transcendence' are not the experiences of the majority of those in the West, even though some involvement in spiritism, the reading of horoscopes, tarot cards, and the consultation of various forms of so-called spiritual healing and clairvoyance, has certainly grown throughout the Western world in recent years. Yet many in the West are touched at certain keys points in their lives by experiences which can be said to raise issues of transcendence.

It is important that we clarify a little more the meaning of the phrase, 'issues of transcendence'. I do not mean to suggest that an 'issue of transcendence' is the same thing as an experience of the God who is transcendent. I mean that there are certain experiences in this life which remind us of our mortality. At one level of our being we all know that we are mortal, and yet at another level we mostly live as if this were not so. Indeed our culture seems to encourage us not to think about such matters. Only occasionally does the possibility of our own finitude impact our thinking in such a way that we become existentially aware of our mortality. A real awareness of our mortality inevitably raises the question of our possible immortality. Alongside questions of mortality and immortality come questions of the meaning of life, of our own significance and value. These are issues of transcendence which do not necessarily bring belief in God, but the question about God is present in these other questions. God, in his transcendence, might be known depending on the answers that we arrive at in facing the questions of transcendence in our own life. For this reason, it is important to be aware that there are a range of very human exeriences which tend to prompt such questions.

1. The rights of passage.   The experience of parenthood brings dramatic changes to the lives of those who are directly involved in caring for a new baby. Many of the questions that are raised are intensely practical. The romance of motherhood and fatherhood is regularly brought into perspective by the cry in the night of the new baby. Changing nappies, dealing with the routine of feeding, facing the financial cost of the new arrival are very immediate questions which cannot be avoided. But alongside such practical considerations, the arrival of a new baby also has the effect of causing parents to ask a whole range of other questions about the purpose of life itself.

The act of procreation raises the issue of our place in creation.

Does this new life have any meaning besides the simple fact of its existence alongside our own? Is the desire to protect, to make sacrifices, to nurture and to consider the future of our offspring, explained entirely by the drive of a species to preserve its own future, or does it point to other issues of transcendence? The fact of a new life does not answer these questions, but it does raise them. The frequent desire to mark the arrival into the world of a baby is an indication of the very human need to attach a significance to this event which speaks of the significance, or sacred nature of life as a whole. That arrival is marked by the naming of a baby. To give a name is to acknowledge significance. It contains the character of a sacred act.

In much the same way, the intention of a couple to share their lives in marriage raises similar questions. The profound commitment to the interests of someone who is other than our own self causes us to ask questions about who we are. How can I be committed to one who is not me? What is the happiness that a couple seek together? What is the basis of the morality that underlies the solemn pledges that are an important element in the marriage service?

The loss of a loved one raises questions about what might lie beyond this life. Even in those cases where a person believes that life is entirely ended by the actuality of physical death, memories remain which are honoured in such a way that we can speak of memories which are sacred. The finality of death seems to draw attention to issues in a relationship which were unresolved in life. When someone dies, the question of the significance of their life is raised in an especially poignant way. By considering the significance of the life of another, we are also asking questions about the significance of our own life.

2. Major Christian festivals.   It is well known that the major Christian festivals either replaced or reflect to some degree older pagan festivals. In their older form these festivals relate in a variety of ways to nature, both in its seasonal aspect (the passage of time), and in its creative function (the growth cycle). Even though only one or two festivals of the church now carry a community significance, originally there were four major festivals, each of which related to the four seasons of the year. Harvest, Christmas, Easter and Whit-suntide. These were not the only festivals, but they were the most important. Even today, much larger numbers of attenders will be present for one or other of these festival occasions, to mark them by their presence, if not with their participation. The act of simply being present is both important and sufficient. Attendance implies belonging without necessitating believing. The need to belong is a response to felt questions; who am I, what is my significance, where do I fit?

3. Prayer.   Roger Edrington's research illustrates the extent to which private prayer, even if secret, is part of a widespread experience amongst individuals. Prayer is one expression of a wider pattern of religious experience. The Alister Hardy Research Centre in Oxford has discovered that in some surveys as many as two thirds of adults in some British cities claim to have had some kind of religious experience which they could remember and which made some impression on them.[10] The common practice of prayer and the memory of other experiences speak of an 'otherness' in life which is rarely expressed in formal religious structures. Such experiences form the basis for a means of expression which enables conversation about transcendence to take place.

4. Moments of crisis.   Many, though not all, of the experiences of 'another' dimension to life come in moments of crisis. Illness, the shock of unemployment, the sudden and unexpected loss of a loved one, an awareness of guilt, the breakdown of a marriage, these and many other crisis experiences sometimes lead to the need to talk about the meaning and effect of these events. 'Why me?' is a question that many clergy have heard in the context of talking about moments of crisis in peoples' lives.

Those who are ministers of religion will know something of the enormous privilege of meeting people in any or all of these circumstances. The minister is often changed by these encounters as much as the lives of those to whom they minister. Dark secrets, splendid joys, the knowledge that one has glimpsed people as they really are, rather than the person that they present to others, these are all moments of intimacy in human relationships. The space that is created by such intimacy allows the transcendent to enter our world. Faith in God is often generated or strengthened at such times.

Ministry and transcendence

We can argue that the power of such events is so great that these encounters represent the major means by which the gospel message of Jesus Christ can be sensitively conveyed. Devoted Christian ministers can meet many hundreds of people in the exercise of their ministry who will come to faith at such times. The opportunity to engage with moments of transcendence is therefore part of the normal pastoral cycle of Christian ministry. But all of these moments are firmly embedded in the territory of that which is somehow religious and is identified to some extent with the world of the church. The very nature of this ministry means that those who experience transcendence in such a way need to come into the orbit of the church to benefit from the occasional offices, counselling, confession or the experience of other sacraments. It is a pastoral ministry which gently invites. But the task of mission means more than issuing an invitation. It also requires the church to meet those to whom mission is directed on their territory, rather than on the hallowed ground of the life of the church. This raises the question as to whether there are places where God breaks in on the secular world which most people inhabit.

Experiences of transcendence in the realm of the secular

1. Friendship.   The need for companionship is basic to who we are as human beings. This reality is reflected in the biblical account of creation. Adam, though he 'walked with God', also needed human companionship. God's creation of Eve was a response to this very basic need. For most of us, being totally alone is a very unpleasant experience. It is this knowledge that makes solitary confinement a punishment and not a blessing in prison life. But companionship by itself does not entirely meet the need of the human condition.

Friendship goes beyond mere companionship. The importance of friendship is reflected in the gospel of John's account of the relationship that Jesus had with his disciples. The high point in that relationship arrives on the occasion of the Last Supper. They had arrived at the place where Jesus wanted his followers to know that they were not just to have a relationship of service with him, meaningful as that might be, but they were to be his friends.

The point about friendship is that those who experience such a relationship know what it is to be loved. The word 'love' in the English language can be a rather weak word. Another way of expressing the content of friendship is to use the more intimate word 'beloved'. Someone who experiences the effect of love in a friendship is one who knows what it is to be beloved. This word conveys the essential, unconditional content of the regard of the friend. It suggests that friendship is offered, not because the one who is loved is particularly deserving of such love, but they are loved out of a quality of generosity. This kind of friendship affirms the basic worth of someone, not because of any obvious gain that comes from this transaction, indeed there may be many unattractive aspects in the character of one who is beloved, but simply because this recognition is freely given without any particular expectation of reward. Life comes to have meaning simply because one is beloved.

The importance of the meaning that is bestowed on life through friendship is illustrated in the extent to which friendship is seen as related to acts of sacrifice. The true friend will risk all to protect the wellbeing of the one who is loved and valued. While one can easily understand a mother acting sacrificially for her children, or a husband for his wife, the capacity of friends to make sacrifices for each other is less easy to comprehend.

In much the same way that friendship can produce great acts of selfless courage, so those same acts, occasionally offered between strangers, can result in the creation of friendship. Sometimes a lifelong bond is created even when there is no opportunity to develop friendship after such an event has taken place. One of the respondents in Roger Edrington's research describes in some detail the action of a fellow soldier who carried him while wounded at great personal cost. He could never forget that act even though he never met the soldier again. It was as if that man's action had bestowed worth and meaning on the life of the one who was saved.[11]

2. The Arts.   It would be foolish to argue that every artistic endeavour, be it visual, written or spoken, is somehow representative of an attempt to grasp the transcendent. Yet there is a case for arguing that this is precisely what great art really is. At the very least, art is an important mirror of the society that produces it. The connection between the world of ideas and the world of literature, sculpture and painting is brilliantly surveyed by the art historian Kenneth Clark in his book *Civilisation*. His presentation of the history of Western art from Rome, through the Dark Ages to the Middle Ages and into the modern world demonstrates clearly the way in which art reflects the prevailing thinking of the day.

Clark recognises the dilemma that faces modern art in the context of the discoveries of Einstein and Rutherford. Having outlined the consequences of the new physics for modern man's understanding of the world, Clark comments that artists:

> ...have always responded instinctively to latent assumptions about the shape of the universe. The incomprehensibility of our new cosmos seems to me, ultimately, to be the reason for the chaos of modern art. I know next to nothing about science, but I've spent my life trying to learn about art, and I am completely baffled by what is taking place today.[12]

So if the arts in general and painting in particular simply reflect the world around us, and if today that reflection only results in a heightened chaos and despair, how can we speak of seeing the transcendent through art? Certainly we can see such transcendence in the art of previous ages. Are we restricted only to a memory of what has been? Is art so much a captive of our present age that it only serves the interests of a heightened immanence?

To a great extent this is true, and even when we turn to literature, both in the form of novels and plays, we see something of the same dilemma. But the arts can never be entirely confined to the role of simply reflecting that which is. Even the art which reflects despair cannot avoid suggesting the question, 'Is this all that life signifies?' Art never finally answers that question, but it does draw the participant, whether as artist or as observer, into an existential encounter with the forces that underly life and death.

By its very nature the world of art acts upon those senses which can never be entirely confined by the philosophical systems which predominate at any particular time. In this sense art drives humanity to a task of creative imagination that presses beyond the world we know, and so asks questions about the world that we do not know.

3. Humour. The church is not often associated with the domain of laughter. Indeed Christians are much more familiar with being laughed at than with the expression of laughter in worship. The church is not alone in being seen as somehow always serious. There is little laughter in any system which claims for itself an ultimate significance. Communist regimes and totalitarianism of all kinds find humour rather uncomfortable. It is very significant that Orwell portrays the world of 1984 as totally lacking in laughter. In his book on the vision of the comic, Conrad Hyers refers to the character in Orwell's 1984, Robert Ketchum. He is presented in the novel as the last person in the United States known to have laughed and was executed for this crime.[113] The absence of joy signifies a dehumanising tendency.

It does not follow that humour always implies a connection with the transcendent. But humour does have some dimensions which are very important in speaking about the creation itself. Conrad Hyers speaks about three levels of humour. First he identifies the laughter of paradise. Such laughter is the innocent childlike level of play unencumbered with double meaning. It is simply a joyful response to being alive. He describes it as 'the world of innocence prior to the knowledge of good and evil'.[114] Secondly there is what Hyers calls the laughter of paradise lost.[115] This level of laughter reflects the fact that good and evil introduce tension into life. It attempts to confront the essential absurdity of life. Thirdly there is the level of paradise regained. Humour of this kind reflects a degree of victory over the absurdity of life. It is the laughter of friendship and intimacy, a laughter which is not unaware of the tensions contained in life, but which has sought to overcome them in a secure and mature relationship.[16]

What connection does humour make with an experience of the transcendent? First, it speaks of hope. The essence of tragedy is that those who are noble are destroyed, almost relentlessly so by the presence of a fatal flaw, either in their own character or through the wiles of those they trust, or even by forces outside of their control. Occasionally, as in the case of Shakespeare's Othello, all three elements conspire to make the unthinkable take place. The death of Desdemona at the hands of Othello defies all reason and logic yet, slowly, horrifyingly, the tragedy unfolds. Goodness comes apart at the seams. Humour, by contrast, is often about the happy ending, despite all indications to the contrary.[17] It represents the triumph of hope against every expectation that disaster waits to strike. The end of many comedies presents some kind of reconciliation. It may be a feast, a marriage or a celebration of some kind. The warring couple, or even the family in conflict, find a peace of some sort. The contradictions of the plot are not fully resolved, but love and forgiveness, peace and grace somehow contrive to put matters right. The end is rarely complete perfection, but it is an ending that allows us to live with imperfection. The foolishness of the human condition does not finally bring destruction. If there are tears at all they are the tears of joy. Romance and comedy are as inseparable as romance and tragedy.

Secondly, humour speaks of the triumph of good over evil. In the play *Godspell*, the person of Jesus is presented as a clown. The text of the play is taken directly from Matthew's gospel. At first the idea of Jesus the clown seems to suggest that the author is mocking the Christ. The contrast with the seriousness of most characterisations of Jesus is almost shocking. Yet the sense of the celebration of life that is conveyed in the gospels is gradually and compellingly transmitted through the image of the clown. The vitality, energy and zest for life that is unmistakably part of the attraction of Jesus is given free rein in Godspell.

But what about the crucifixion? Can the image of a clown really bear the weight of such a momentous confrontation with evil? The presentation of the resurrection in *Godspell* is not necessarily obvious and explicit. But the crucifixion itself is more important than simply to act as a necessary prerequisite for the resurrection. By demonstrating that evil is present in life and that life is more of a tragi-comedy than just a comedy alone, the play conveys a strong sense of the way that life really is. This is not a sugar and spice story of difficulties that somehow works out alright in the end, simply because the hero muddles through to some fortunate conclusion. The reality of the resurrection is present throughout the whole event. The strength of the clown as compared with the malevolent, but essential weakness of evil, suggests that good will triumph because it is intrinsically stronger than evil. Humour, therefore, allows us to face the tragedy of life head on and survive because it points to the existence of forces in the universe that are in principal stronger than evil.

Thirdly, humour presents the essential mystery of life. There is a difference between life as mysterious and life as inexplicable. The latter view can easily lead to a perspective which sees life not as humourous but as a cruel joke played on humankind. There is no real humour in the cruel hoax played by one who has a terrible last laugh. Life is difficult to understand, yet its essential mystery can be approached by seeing the paradoxes that are present in many aspects of our existence. These paradoxes can be painful. Humour allows us to face the potential absurdity of life and emerge with a sense of wonder rather than despair.[18]

The potential humour contained in a paradox points us to a meaning which lies beyond the pain of the ingredients contained within the paradox. Religion which pretends to explain the meaning of life, but which does not also see the absurdity contained within the human condition, always falls short of an adequate explanation. In taking itself too seriously religion fails to accomplish its true purpose. The true God is always the God of surprises, who manages to escape the firm categories of any religious system. Humour reminds us of this true God and so allows us to experience a sense of awe and wonder that is at the same time capable of apprehension, even if not of comprehension.

4. The role of the narrative.   Theologians have become very used to talking of narrative theology in recent years. The presentation of Jesus as a master of narrative, as a storyteller of excellence, has received a great deal of attention in such circles. The revival of interest in storytelling extends beyond the world of theology. In the United Kingdom, the strangely named 'Crick-Crack Club' has attempted to promote traditional adult tales. Their literature surveys the extent to which the resurgence of storytelling has become a worldwide phenomenon. They comment:

> Traditional oral narratives range from bawdy jokes to sacred epic myth. In the past this shared ancestral heritage reached from village hearths to royal courts.[19]

At one level, the storyteller is an entertainer. The Crick-Crack Club recommends twelve 'professional' storytellers who have built up an expertise in speaking to public audiences. But the role of narrative is important for reasons which go beyond this very 'lo-tech' form of entertainment.

Thomas Boomershine has worked extensively in the area of storytelling and makes a fascinating connection between the English word 'gospel' and the medium of story. He suggests that the etymology of the word gospel can be traced as follows:

> Gospel is a shortened form of an Old English word, 'godspell.' It means: 'god' good, 'spell' tale i.e. 'good tale.' A spell was a spoken word or set of words believed to have magic power. In Old English, therefore, the word that was the best equivalent for the Latin word, evangelium, was a tale whose telling had power.[20]

The history of the West has been particularly influenced by the gospel story as a single entity and by particular stories in the Bible. Other stories, both ancient and modern, that come to us from a variety of other sources have also become familiar themes in the telling of stories remembered from childhood. Why is it that a good story becomes a tale 'whose telling has power', and what is the nature of that power?

First, it is important to remember that a story which is told is not the same thing as a story presented in the form of a novel. The story in a novel might be a very attractive and powerful story, but it is not easily presented orally. As Boomershine notes,[21] the story which is told deals with the language of experience. It has the same structure as our experience.

Secondly, unlike the essentially private experience of reading a novel, storytelling involves face-to-face encounter. The audience comes to know something of the storyteller as well as the story. In most situations the audience will respond to the story. Their laughs and gasps will encourage or possibly stimulate the storyteller to shape his tale in a particular way. In this way the audience will reveal its own unique characteristics to the storyteller.

Thirdly, the form of personal interaction that takes place between storyteller and audience has the capacity to go beyond friendship to create a sense of community. As Boomershine also notes, 'There is something about a good story that virtually demands retelling.'[22] The process of retelling creates a wider network which has a shared knowledge and response. Clearly, if a story is perceived to deal with very significant issues and ideas, so the degree of identification intensifies. That identification can become so strong that communities are formed as a response to the message of the story. Those communities may be very loosely connected in terms of sharing certain cultural values, or they may take organisational forms as they attempt to express the meaning of the story through lifelong commitments.

Fourthly, the good story tells us something about who we are. It reflects our hopes, struggles, fears and moments of sadness. The good story becomes our story. We enter into the story and shape it so that it helps to meet our needs. The very telling of a story can confirm that we are part of a wider family which knows something of our story. The values, hopes and aspirations of that broader family, or community, are reinforced by the telling of a story. There can be feelings of pride and wonder which remind us that what went before makes us who we are, and so allows us to be part of that community of experience made familiar by the retelling of a common story. Many nations have such stories which help them to understand and define their national identity. These stories may be so well known by the members of a nation that they will not always be recognised as stories. The details of such stories will almost certainly not be known to those outside the nation.

So the story has a number of important functions in relation to issues of transcendence. First, it implicitly suggests that there is meaning in life. Secondly, it makes some suggestion as to what that meaning might be, not by philosophical debate, but by eulogising certain values and behaviour patterns exhibited by the hero of the story. Thirdly, it invites the listener to evaluate their own life story in relation to the story that is told. The story gives significance to the life story of the listener. Their life experience can be equated with the experience recounted in the story. It is not just that the themes of significant stories abound with explicit questions about life and death, but at a deeper level they suggest to the listener that the meaning or story of each person's life can be grasped by apprehending the deeper meaning of the larger story, or what some have called the 'metanarrative'.

But such a conclusion represents something of a problem for our modern world. There is an absence of such stories. That is part of the crisis of our culture. In our present times the place of testimony (what is true for me), often takes the place of the broader story. But the importance of testimony – the telling of personal experience – at least indicates that our culture is searching for stories. The compelling testimony offers a link with the wider story of humanity – what might be true for another might help me to understand what is true more widely.

Secularising the transcendent

If it is the case that the challenge of the transcendent constantly emerges even in a thoroughly secular landscape, how does that help those who have a concern for the Christian message? It is all too possible for the transcendent to become trivialised. The pressure of a secular world-view acts to persuade us to forget our dreams and visions, or at least to accept an account of meaning that is so obsessed with answering the question 'how?' that we have come to think that it is the same thing as the question 'why?' Some reactions to modernity have trivialised our experience of the transcendent by confusing it with an enhanced immanence.

The temptation for Christians to respond to experiences of secular transcendence with new evangelistic methods is all too likely to develop and all too certain to fail. Even now I am reading books which give instruction on how, (that dreaded word again), to reach secular people. It is not that these are bad books, indeed some are very insightful and I find myself agreeing with most of the perspectives that many of these books outline. The problem lies in our potential reaction to such books. If we come to see them as instruction manuals that provide a methodology, then they will have failed in their purpose. It will not be enough for the church to remain largely unchanged and to seek instead to simply add a few useful communication tools. It would be even worse if we concluded that what we really need is to encourage forms of Christian art, the creation of an exclusively Christian humour, and the recruitment of Christian storytellers. The task facing the church is much more fundamental.

New forms of western churches

In describing experiences of transcendence in the secular realm, what I am suggesting is not a method by which people can be converted to Christianity, so much as pointing to a language which can be shared by those who stand inside the Christian community and those who stand outside of it. The new task of the church is to learn both to speak and live such a language. The learning of such a language causes the church to become a very different kind of institution. In a number of places in the Western world, new forms of the church are beginning to emerge. In vastly different ways they are beginning to meet with secular people on their territory. Three examples illustrate this process.

1. Church for the unchurched.   A network of churches inspired by the initiative of Willow Creek Community Church, Chicago, has emerged over the last ten years. Willow Creek is reputedly the fastest growing Protestant church in North America and is now the second largest church in the United States. But it is not its size that is important so much as its attempt to answer the question, 'What would a church look like if it was designed for those who don't come, rather than for those who do come?' As you might expect, the practical result of creating such a church has produced a very different kind of institution from that with which most Christians will be familiar.

The weekend worship service is known as a 'Seeker's Service'. The ingredients in this event are closer to that of a theatre than a church. Drama and music serve to introduce the sermon. The structure of the sermon is radically different from that which features in most Christian worship services. It begins with a 'life issue' rather than a Bible text and strongly features personal narrative as the major form of communication. Humour and the arts are used creatively to raise awareness of these key issues in the lives of those who attend. It is not that the Bible and an orthodox understanding of the Christian faith are unimportant to this church. It is simply that the heart of the church takes place outside of the weekend worship services. These 'services' are simply a means of presenting a credible apologetic for the faith in a setting which those from a secular mind-set can accept as 'their turf'.[23]

Despite its innovative approach, the original 'Willow Creek' model still feels very much like a church to those from a European context. The imitators of Willow Creek in Europe have departed significantly from the detail of the model and are often attempting to create models for exploring faith which are much more avowedly secular in their feel. The heart of all these attempts is not slick marketing so much as the encouraging of the Christian community to build genuine friendships with unchurched, secular people in the natural social settings where everyday life is lived.

2. Shifting the paradigms. The 'Vineyard' network of churches inspired by John Wimber's Vineyard Community Church in California has pioneered a rather different model for communicating with the secular mind-set. The heart of this model strongly advocates the demonstration of 'signs and wonders' in the context of a worship experience, combined with the building of personal relationships in what are known as 'kinship groups'. The 'signs and wonders' spoken of by the Vineyard network refer to manifestations of the power of the Holy Spirit in such areas as prayer for healing, and other phenemona frequently associated with the Pentecostal movement.

The conviction of Wimber is that secular people need to undergo a 'paradigm shift' which allows them to move outside of a purely secular world-view in order to hear the Christian message.[24] The actual experience of a biblical world-view is seen as important in allowing people to hear the Christian message through the blinkers which a secular mind-set imposes. (Wimber sees this as important for secularised christians as much as for secularised non-christians). The setting in which such experiences take place is thoroughly contemporary in terms of the music, language and social setting.

Although at first sight the approach of the Vineyard communities and that of Willow Creek seem to be radically different, there are more similarities than initially seem evident. There is a strong argument which suggests that these two approaches build on a very similar framework, but one which is highly contextualised given the very different settings of an innovative Californian life-style and that of corporate Chicago.

3. Exploring spirituality. The work of the Taizé community in France, together with very similar approaches to worship associated with groups in Britain such as the Iona Community, represents an attempt to explore a very simple approach to spirituality. These long-term experiments have attracted large numbers of people for whom traditional church life seems to be inaccessible.

Taizé is noteworthy for its strongly affirmative view of the created order, of sexuality, of art and beauty, of meditative silence, and of simple contemporary music in its liturgies. These world-affirming ingredients are used to point to a sense of otherness which can be experienced in the midst of our secular experience.

The re-emergence of these more ancient themes can be observed in a number of other expressions unconnected with the Taizé community itself. In recent years, pilgrimages to ancient Christian centres have become popular, even with those who hold no obvious religious faith at all. Retreat centres have been attracting more and more of those who find traditional Christian practice and belief difficult and remote. It is as if the church is being recreated amongst secular people beyond the normal boundaries of the church.

I do not mean to suggest that the approaches of Willow Creek, Vineyard or Taizé are mutually exclusive experiments. It is not the case that Taizé explores spirituality and the other two do not. Nor is it the case that Willow Creek majors on friendship while the examples of Taizé and the Vineyard do not. Far from it. The overlap between these three expressions of the church are considerable. Indeed it has been fascinating to watch how many local churches are interested in all three of these developments and attempt to incorporate lessons from each of these insights and from other developments beside.

One example of such integration is that of the Thomasmass begun in Helsinki.[25] As the name suggests, it is a mass held for those with real doubts. Its approach is to be seeker-friendly and yet the strongly liturgical style and content borrows very heavily from the Taizé tradition. Many of those who began this movement are involved in the Charismatic movement and would be very comfortable with the thinking and practice of John Wimber. It is clear that many of those whose souls have been torn, those who are very like the lonely men of Edrington's study, are finding healing and help in such a context. Indeed the Thomasmass is particularly noted for the very high numbers of men who attend this event.

Nor are these illustrations an exhaustive survey of the renewal of the church. They are simply indications of a vast change that has the potential to transform the ways in which the Christian community, and those outside of that community, communicate with each other. The meeting place is no longer exclusively the territory of the church so much as those points of transcendence that reflect something of God's activity in the world. This does not mean that the church can afford to be complacent. The changes which are alluded to are very new and it is by no means certain what the future will hold. But we can be sure that although these developments offer hope for the church in its engagement with mission in the West, some very significant questions remain to be faced by the whole Christian community.

CHAPTER TEN

LIGHTING THE BEACON

The growing recognition that the West represents the most recent and the most challenging mission field in the world for the Christian faith is accompanied by a growing crisis in Christian mission generally.[1] In part, the crisis is related to the single fact that missions have traditionally been directed to the two-thirds world from the Christian West, whereas today the centre of Christianity is in Africa. The missionary movement is now a very complex enterprise. Brazilian churches are sending missionaries to former Portuguese colonies in Africa. Africans are attempting cross-cultural missions within their own continent. Indian Christians from the South of India, and from such tribal areas as Nagaland, are evangelising the Hindu heartlands of North India. Still other Asians from the Indian sub-continent are deliberately planning and planting churches amongst the Asian diaspora. Christians in other South East Asian lands are sending missionaries to other lands within the same region. Indeed, there is a sizeable missionary movement operating from this increasingly active two-thirds world to the West.

It is possible to argue that some of these changes derive from the very success of the missionary movement in producing healthy, indigenous churches in other parts of the world. But it is also true that the crisis derives in part from the intellectual crisis facing the Western world. The sense that the modern era is passing, but has not yet been replaced by any other dominant world view, underscores the questions that face missions in general and mission in the West particularly.

The missiologist David Bosch has pointed to the work of the theologian Hans Kung who has described the history of the church as falling into six distinct epochs. Bosch adds that these six categories apply not only to church history in general, but also to the missionary experience and strategy of the church.[2] The categories quoted by Bosch are as follows:

1. The apocalyptic paradigm of primitive Christianity
2. The Hellenistic paradigm of the patristic period.
3. The medieval Roman Catholic period.
4. The Protestant (Reformation) paradigm.
5. The modern Enlightenment paradigm.
6. The emerging ecumenical paradigm.

Each of these periods interpreted the faith in particular ways. In part this was because each period was interested in very different questions, but it is also true that the world-view of these periods was sufficiently different that each one operated with a different paradigm. From the perspective of Bosch, each epoch had a very different understanding of the mission of the church. Moreover, the transition from one epoch to another was never an easy matter. More often than not these huge changes were accompanied by tribulation and conflict. None of these transitions took place overnight.

It is vital to note that Küng's sixth paradigm shift has not yet taken place, it is only now emerging. The church, together with Western culture, finds itself caught between two ages. This is both a painful and a confusing place in which to be. This confusion explains in part the seeming inability of the church to understand and direct its contemporary mission in the West.

It is easy to look back on past periods and see clearly the questions that the church wrestled with then. The first century Christians had to ask the critical missionary question, 'Can Gentiles become Christians without becoming Jews?' The early church fathers were occupied with the demanding intellectual task of intepreting Christianity in the context of Greek philosophy and thought. Each period had its own questions which are now very clear to us. However, the questions were nowhere near as clear to those who found themselves caught between any two at the time. Clarity only emerged later. Therefore, it is likely that there will be a lack of clarity for those of us caught between the paradigms of the Enlightenment and that which is to follow. It is by no means certain that Küng's phrase 'the ecumenical paradigm' will be the one which will become attached to the new period which is even now bringing itself to bear on our time. But even though it might be difficult to see clearly the exact content of the missionary questions that the church will have to face in its contemporary mission, it is important to begin the process of suggesting what the new agenda might be. Three questions confront this author as critical issues.

What is the message?

I am not suggesting that Christians either can, or should, change the content of the Christian message to suit a new audience as if they were simply latter-day Marcionites. Indeed it is worth reaffirming the degree of agreement that scholars as far apart theologically as C. H. Dodd and John Stott are able to reach concerning the content of the apostolic preaching. Stott agrees with Dodd when he asserts that the basic content of apostolic preaching as reflected in the gospels can be summarised as:[3]

1. The events surrounding the gospel proclamation.
2. The witnesses, (including the prophets), of the gospel.
3. The affirmations, or claims of the gospels.
4. The promises contained in the gospel.
5. The response demanded by the gospel from those who hear it.

But even though Christians of every age might agree with each other about the content of the Christian message, the way in which that content is interpreted and applied has certainly varied enormously depending on the context in which the message has been preached. Indeed some thinkers have even wondered if the variation of expression has been so great that it is difficult to claim that it is always the same message![4] It is not our purpose to enter that debate so much as to begin to ask how the content of the faith might be communicated in an understandable framework to those who are part of the coming world view.

The communication of the Christian story has at least three variable aspects.

1. The issue of emphasis.   Not every aspect of the apostolic preaching is always given equal emphasis. This reality is recognised in the world of Bible translation. The scarcity of resource compared with the huge cost of Bible translation work often means that the whole Bible will not be translated into a new language. Instead, the workers on the field will recommend that a particular book or part of the Bible will be translated first. The choice of book will often reveal a great deal about the perception of the missionaries as to which parts of the apostolic preaching are the most important in the context in which they are working. Sometimes these choices seem to be very surprising.

For example, whereas most missionaries initially request the translation of one or other of the gospels, those who were working with one particular people group requested a translation of the book of Genesis. This had little to do with the fact that Genesis is the first book of the Bible so much as the fact that Genesis includes the story of the creation of the world. The people group in question had their own creation story, but it was one which caused this people to have a very low regard for their own origins. The message that there was an alternative explanation of their beginning was a very attractive notion. In this case, the story of creation authenticated in a very powerful manner the gospel story that these people had already heard. The story of creation became a powerful 'witness' to the gospel. The identification of the people with this story allowed them also to become witnesses of the truth of the gospel message, in the sense that the central affirmations of the gospel were given a powerful and immediate meaning. It is not that gospel events, promises and demands were never mentioned, but the central issue became the linkage between the witnesses to the gospel and the affirmations contained in the gospel.

2. The importance of context.   The questions that the gospel is seen to address will vary in relation to the context of the preaching. The questions that occupied the medieval period were very different to those at the heart of our own age. The fundamental concern of medieval society was to ask the question, what does it mean to have a Christian society? This central question gave rise to questions about order and stability, rights and responsibilities, duty and honour, charity and goodness, just wars and justice. These caused Christians to view the parables, for example, in relation to their moral content because it was questions about social behaviour that were being asked.

We may scorn the vision of a society which saw it as a priority to cover the land with church buildings so that one would always be able to see a church spire. This physical reminder of the agenda of the medieval world is a long way from the agenda of a society which is more concerned with the number of fridges, cars, telephones, televisions and video recorders in each home. But the central question of society has changed. Our own time is more likely to ask the question, can the human race survive? This rather urgent question gives a very different cutting edge to the way in which the gospel message is applied. In our century, the eschatological content of many of the parables of Jesus has been underscored. The teaching of Jesus is recognised not only to have a moral content, but a prophetic kernal, warning of the destruction of our world.

3. The use of analogy.   The analogies that are used to explain the message necessarily change. The problems of communicating the message of the Bible across cultures are many and varied. What do you do if a society values deceit rather than truth? In such a setting the story of Jesus and Judas is heard in exactly the wrong way. Judas is the hero and Jesus a fool if not actually the villain of the piece.

The essentially agrarian context of the Bible works well for many societies, but the nuances of the stories are lost to an industrial audience. Knowledge of the Old Testament is essential to make any sense of a phrase such as 'the Lamb of God'. What would a Sri Lankan, Tamil audience make of that? They might understand how someone could be a tiger, but hardly a lamb! I remember trying to explain the content of 1 Corinthians Chapter 12 to a welder who built Land Rovers. He had great difficulty understanding Paul's imagery of the church as the body of Christ. Eventually a light dawned. 'Oh,' he said, 'now I get it, you mean the church is like the parts of a lathe.' Actually, I wasn't sure if I meant that or not, but once he had explained how a lathe worked, I was more certain we were talking the same language.

So, given these variables, how can we begin to think about the Christian message in the Western world? What elements will be important for twentieth-century people living in the chasm between modernity and post-modernity? What are the concerns of those who are unchurched? What aspect of the Christian messsage speaks to their situation?

For the past six to seven years I have worked for the British and Foreign Bible Society. A large part of my job has involved travelling and speaking to individuals and groups about the mission of the church. During this time I have always been interested to know what it was that influenced someone to become a Christian. Occasionally I have asked particular audiences if anyone became a Christian from a totally unchurched background. I have generally been surprised at how many people have been converted to the Christian faith from an unchurched background, especially in more recent years. Whenever I have asked this question, I have tried to engage in some dialogue, especially by asking the question, what was there about the Christian message that attracted and interested you? I have asked the question in this way because I am not just interested in the process by which someone becomes a Christian, although this is also a legitimate area of interest. As you might imagine the responses to such a question are rather varied. A few individuals gave answers which were entirely unexpected to me, and ones which I had never heard from anyone else. These were by definition uniquely personal factors. But the clear majority in these informal dialogues has almost always given answers which point clearly to the fact that the Christian story brought meaning to the story of their lives.

In one sense this finding is hardly startling. Indeed, when I have mentioned this conclusion to colleagues, a good number have indicated that they would have expected such a response. But viewed in another way it is a significant response for two quite different reasons. First, it stands in contrast to the kinds of concerns that motivated people to become Christians in previous times. We do not find the kind of anguished concern to know what happens beyond the grave that the Victorians seemed to exhibit. Nor do we see a concern with issues of hell, judgement and damnation such as we see in earlier ages. It is unlikely that those who have become Christians in the West in recent years would either have produced, or have been inspired, by Dante's portrait of hell. The anxiety which produces the modern God encounter is not just a personal concern with identity – who am I? – but more a question of how the I that I am relates meaningfully to the world in which such people live. In talking to those who have significant contact with unchurched people, it seems that the issues that arise again and again are not so much issues of identity, but rather questions that emerge from the primary relationships of life – marriage, the family and the workplace.

Secondly, it brings us to the major point of contention that stands at the centre of the crisis of the culture of the West. At the very centre of modernity lies a story of the nature of reality, sometimes referred to as a metanarrative (or grand story), which is in direct conflict with the metanarrative of the Christian gospel.[5] That story includes a belief in man and his inevitable progress. The theory of evolution is itself adapted to indicate that this progress not only uses science to bring progress into being, but is itself a scientific fact of our existence. Hope for secular man does not lie in the vicissitudes of nature, or in the will of a distant god, but in the hands of an enlightened modern man, who, given time, will bring in the Utopia previously associated with the coming Kingdom of God. The deaths of millions in our century at the hands of men, fired not by religious conviction but by ideological fervour and personal vanity, have helped to bring such a metanarrative into question. To express it more starkly, the original driving metanarrative of modernity is intellectually bankrupt. The power of scientific methodology remains. The question is whether another metanarrative will emerge to give direction to that methodology.

The claim of post-modernism is that such a metanarrative will not emerge because there cannot be such a grand story. According to post-modern thinkers, the new reality is that there is no metanarrative. Therefore it is not a question of whether the competing stories of modernity or Christianity, or of any other system, is true or not; they are all equally untrue because there simply cannot be any such story by which our world, its past, its present and its future can be understood. However, there are those who claim that the very assertion that there is no metanarrative itself represents a form of metanarrative and, moreover, that the basic forms of this post-modern metanarrative contain a veiled violence.[6] The assertion that our world has no meaning is a very committed statement. It certainly goes far beyond not knowing whether our world has meaning or not, or not knowing what that meaning is. This represents a new opportunity for Christianity. The argument that there is enough order in the world to suggest that meaning does exist is a very strong one indeed.

The new challenge for the Christian message is to explain clearly how the Christian metanarrative offers a convincing explanation of the meaning of life. In the meantime, the confusion that surrounds the issue of life's meaning results in a quest for some interim certainties, especially concerning morality. One of the staff members of a notable North American church, well known for its relationship with unchurched people, has written about those connections.[7] He lists fifteen observations concerning the unchurched people he has met, many of whom are his friends. The list very obviously divides into two kinds of concerns. Those which indicate a basic skepticism that the church has a message worth hearing, and those which are concerned to find a message which will give direction, meaning and authenticity to life. The search for morality is both commendable and understandable. Ultimately, morality without a broadly agreed metanarrative has little or no basis.

What kind of community?

The evidence of the book of Acts indicates that the first Christian community had a distinctive life style. The believers worshipped every day in the temple and held their possessions in common. There is little evidence to suggest that either of these practices survived beyond the first few years of the Jerusalem church. But even though these specific manifestations of community did not continue, it is obvious that during the first few centuries of its life, the church was clear about its 'called out' nature. It was distinct from society. Persecution helped Christians to experience the cost and distinctiveness of the community that was the church. The nature of that community was severely tested, not only during persecution, but also after particular persecutions ended. How would the church regard those members of the community who had not been able to withstand persecution and who had apostatised?

The eventual emergence of the church as the dominant religious force in Western society brought a very different relationship between the community of the church and society as a whole. What did it mean to belong to the church when virtually everyone in society was also a baptised member of the church? It is not surprising that a broadly Christian society produced a variety of specialised religious communities whose wider function was to help the constant reform and renewal of the whole Christian community. One can argue that the Reformation itself was partly a response to the tension between the need for the church to be distinct from society and yet also be in relationship with that same society. The anabaptist concept of the believers church, (sometimes called the gathered church), emphasised the idea that the church needed to be seen as a voluntary community, distinct in some respects from society as a whole.

The ending of the concept and the social reality of Christendom brought a very confused situation for the Christian church. The emergence of the secular state, which replaced the supposed monolith of Christendom, has produced a sharp division between the Christian community and society, even, and some would argue especially, in those situations where there is a strong State church. In the modern world, there has come a strong undercurrent which argues that the church should attend only to the world of private religious commitment and that the State should attend to all matters of public policy. Morality and belief, therefore, become a matter of private conviction and not a matter of State legislation. In such a world, the private and the public do not meet.

The modern world rejects the intrusion of the church into public education, economics, social and industrial policy and, increasingly, into public morality. The secular State necessarily rejects the idea that there are any moral absolutes that stem from divine revelation. The guiding principles for the State lie instead in the supposed reasoned absolutes of the Enlightenment – freedom, equality and the pursuit of happiness through material provision for its citizens. The State does not talk so much about morals as it does about values. The only legitimate area for the influence of the church is to attend to the private beliefs and morals of those who are the voluntary members of the various Christian churches.

What does it mean to be the Christian community in a secular state? The Christian community must be honest and admit that it has lost the intellectual high ground. It is primarily for this reason that the church has had to accept the terms offered to it by the secular authorities – the freedom to pursue religious activities in private. In a situation where the public values of the State are largely drawn from the inherited Christian culture of the past, the church can accept its new role without noticing that anything much has changed. Public life goes on much as before. The status, place and perceived utilitarian value of the churches change little from the time when Christian revelation formed the culture. But increasingly society in the West has challenged the accepted Christian norms of the past, increasingly so in the area of family and sexuality. The traditional Christian view is defended by those who have a gut feeling that such an inheritance is preferable to the new norms that are being introduced, but the intellectual foundation of such a defence is very weak indeed. There is an attempt to demonstrate that these 'traditional' values have a greater utilitarian value, that is to say that their maintenance is in the best interests of society. But even if such a defence can be proved, it is often only proved once the damage of other values has already been wrought on society.

How has the church responded to this privatised existence? It has to be said that the majority of Christian churches in the West are not the most exciting places in which to be. The composition of the membership of the Christian community does not reflect the general population. The age profile of many European churches is tilted heavily towards older people. The young, especially those in their teens and early twenties, are notable by their absence. The working classes in Europe have largely deserted the church. Far more women than men attend church. If the Christian message brings joy to those who believe, then such a reality is often difficult to detect simply by attending worship services. A significant number of congregations in the West are very small. In Britain, 50% of all Methodist churches have less than 25 people in attendance each Sunday. The church in the West does not seem to be making a great deal of impact beyond the boundaries of those who have always attended.

Clearly there are many exceptions to this rather gloomy and defeatist portrayal. The most vigorous of local churches do show remarkable signs of community life. Although the public perception and frequent reality might reveal many thousands of very small churches, many of which struggle to maintain their existence, one can also report the presence of many thousands of large and active churches all across the Western world. Even in the highly secular landscape of Europe, there are those city churches which have more than a thousand worshippers on a Sunday. These 'megachurches' can demonstrate their utilitarian value to the families who attend. Imaginative youth programmes, Sunday School classes, social welfare projects, and even well-equipped gymnasiums all indicate a lively and even muscular approach to the Christian life. Many such churches are adept at gaining new members with sometimes fairly aggressive approaches to evangelism.

But however fulfilling life might be within such Christian complexes, it is difficult to escape the feeling that those who are part of church life are living highly compartmentalised lives. The values taught in church are not those which are recognised in corporate, industrial life. In practice, it is often very difficult for those who are in industry, politics, commerce and education to carry Christian principles into the marketplace. In such circumstances, morality is often highly personal. Christians are placed in a position where their witness to a different world-view is restricted to the often limited impact of their personal integrity, but are not permitted to influence wider public policy. The opportunity to challenge the world-view and assumptions that lie behind public decisions is not very great.

The inescapable question for those who attend church in this privatised context is simply this, 'Does being a Christian only affect one's personal life, or does it make any difference at all to the world in which we live?' The traditional response of a privatised church is to indicate that it will make a difference when the majority of people attend church. There are serious grounds for doubting that this is really so. There does not seem to be much difference in the public policy of governments in Ireland, France and the United States, despite very different levels of church attendance in each of these countries. The dominant driving force in each of these lands is clearly that of a secular world view. Levels of church attendance hardly affect such realities. Certainly the Roman Catholic church in Ireland has been able to exert some influence in the emotive area of abortion, but it is difficult to find many other areas of public policy where forces such as the 'moral majority' have made much significant long-term difference.

Is there any alternative for the Christian community but to accept the increasingly marginalised position offered to it by a secular State? There have been some religious communities, both within Christianity and within other faith positions, notably Judaism, which have advocated a complete withdrawal from all public life. Such groups have created their own society. Not only have they attempted to have as little contact with society as possible in any social sense, they have often developed their own structures of employment and education. Contact with the secular State is limited and grudging. There is no interest in changing society, only in avoiding contact with it. The most extreme examples of such communities often come into conflict with the legal system of the secular State and give every indication of not recognising the validity of secular authority over their lives.

But even in these cases, the ability to live without reference to the rest of society depends crucially on the hope of seeing a new society created by God. They may look to a very temporal solution (as in the case of Jewish sects), to the creation of a religious State outside of the boundaries of the society in which they find themselves. If such a prospect does not seem realisable, there is often a strongly apocalyptic strain in their thought. The imminent return of God is a familiar theme in such communities. Such a return will not only presage the establishment of a new order, it will also include the exercise of judgement over the sins of the outside world. Without the realistic hope of a temporal solution, communities with a strong expectation of the imminent judgement of God tend either to reduce their expectations or self-destruct.

The decision to separate entirely from the world has always manifested itself in the Christian tradition at times of stress, but it has never been the final word of the Christian community. But neither is it possible for the Christian community to live forever with a privatised existence. The Christian gospel contains the assertion that the revelation of God in Jesus Christ is true, not just for those who are believers, but for all of the created order. The heart of the conflict between the church of the first three centuries and the secular State of Rome was that Jesus was Lord, not merely of the church, still less of the private religious experience of believers, but of the whole world. It was the refusal of the early church to abandon this conviction by declaring that Ceasar was Lord in the public sphere that attracted the wrath of Rome.

The church in the West is being reminded by the church in other parts of the world of the need to rediscover the integrity of the Christian message by refusing to accept its status as private truth alone. At the same moment the church in the West is increasingly aware that the church elsewhere in the world is likely to face pressure to accept the status of Christianity as private truth because a secular world-view continues to be exported around the world.

Therefore the Christian community throughout the world stands at a critical crossroads. It is prompted by its own message to both live as though its message is publically true, and to argue for the public truth of that same message. Both will be important. It is not enough to live as though the message is publically true, but not to argue for its truth. The intellectual high ground must be tackled. Neither will it be sufficient to argue for the public truth of the Christian faith without also living as if it is true.

My observation of the growing renewal of the church in the West indicates that it is much more likely that the church will live as if its message is true, without worrying too much about winning the intellectual high ground. Perhaps, surprisingly, in view of the investment of the church in education, the church seems to produce more activists than thinkers. Such a response will undoubtably produce more troops on the ground, but their effectiveness will inevitably be limited unless the strategic high ground is also won.

The Christian community that seeks to engage in both these tasks will be an exciting and, at times, uncomfortable place in which to be. Exciting because the Christian faith will be seen to tackle the issues that will make a difference to our world. Uncomfortable because there is such a long way to go. The early stages of such an endeavour will illicit much more ridicule than it will agreement.

Such a process will inevitably raise the issue of authority. On what authority do Christians make the claims of faith? By the same token, Christians will inevitably need to ask the same question of those who wish to assert the validity of other truth claims. Such a process will lead to a re-examination of the faith claims of competing world views. And that is what they are. The former notion that it is only religious claims that depend on faith statements, in contrast to the certitudes of science, is increasingly being challenged. The essential faith element of all forms of knowing is gradually being recognised. Uncomfortable as it might be for the Christian community, and it almost certainly is uncomfortable, the place of the Bible in understanding the Christian revelation will need to be reconsidered.

What place for the bible?

In a remarkable paper delivered to an annual meeting of biblical scholars held at Manchester College, Oxford, in 1993, Dan Beeby suggested that the time had come for the church to reclaim the Bible from the hands of professional academics. His paper provoked sufficient interest for the issue to appear on the agenda for the 1994 meeting. Since Beeby was speaking to professional academics, his suggestion was deliberately polemical and contained a much more complex argument about the position of Scripture in the Christian community.

The Bible as Scripture.   Beeby makes the point that the term 'Bible'and the term 'Scripture' were at one time used interchangeably, but that they are not used so today. The term 'Bible' is an objective description of a particular book, or more accurately a collection of sixty-six books which can be studied in much the same way as any other significant piece of literature. But to call something 'Scripture' is rather different. That implies commitment. It suggests that this collection of writings has an authority which is somehow different from other powerful works of literature – the power of outstanding literature resides in its art and not in its inherent authority.

When the Bible is understood, not as Scripture, but simply as important literature, then it becomes the property of the university and is viewed in its historical perspective in relation to all other literature. Such a treatment, argues Beeby, does not allow the Bible to be properly understood. It is not merely literature, it is Scripture, and as such can only really be understood in the light of the faith of the church. Christians acknowledge that the Bible is partly the creation of the church, but they also claim that it is the creation of God. It is not just the word of the church, it is the Word of God. As the Word of God, it needs to be seen as a unity. That unity flows from its essentially Christocentric and Trinitarian nature. It is not that the Scripture is a creed. There are few credal statements in Scripture beyond that of saying, 'Jesus is Lord'. However, the creeds are the key to understanding the content of the Scripture because they truly reflect the faith of the church, and that faith is dependent on the revelation of God proclaimed in the pages of the Bible.

As we might expect, Beeby points to the role of the Enlightenment in bringing a separation between the concepts of Bible and Scripture. The Bible still exists, but it no longer acts as Scripture, as foundational truth for Western culture. Having rejected the Bible as the basis of public truth, the new disciplines of the Enlightenment sought to act as the judge of the Bible. The methodology of the university, historical criticism, was brought to bear on the truth of the Bible, and judged according to these norms, the Bible was not only considered to be unworthy of its former status as the authority for public truth, it was also found to be inaccurate, untrustworthy and fundamentally flawed. The critics of the Bible wanted to suggest that the Bible was not only unfit to act as a basis for public truth, it did not deserve to be the basis for private truth either. If faith existed at all, it would have to do so in opposition to reason. It would almost certainly be a blind faith, dependent on prejudice, appealing only to the weak and feeble-minded.

Evangelicals and liberals.   As most Christians will be aware, the church has been tragically divided in its response to such attacks. The most serious division has not been between Catholics and Protestants, or even between the various Protestant denominations, but between those schools of thought that we have somewhat loosely called, 'evangelicals' and 'liberals'. These are somewhat unfortunate labels, and as with most labels do not do justice to the spectrum of positions that thinking Christians have held. However, these terms do indicate a broad differentiation of approach which can be summarised as a 'liberal' position, which has sought relevance for the faith in the modern world, and an 'evangelical' position, which has sought to protect truth from the onslaught of the modern world.

The battleground between liberals and evangelicals has been the question of the authority of the Bible. It was, above all, the emergence of modern critical scholarship that produced these two camps. Certainly there were those who were evangelicals and those who belonged to other groups in church life before controversies over biblical authority came into evidence, but it has been the reactions to German biblical scholarship which has defined the debate in the twentieth century. The early period of the twentieth century was marked by a strong divergence of view. Those who were in the liberal camp tended to embrace warmly the historical critical method. Evangelicals almost uniformly rejected modern scholarship and by doing so became ghettoised. The latter half of the twentieth century has seen a good deal more convergence. Evangelicals have become thoroughly involved in the task of biblical scholarship, often becoming acknowledged leaders in their field. Liberal scholars have been more ready to recognise some problems with the earlier methodologies that had been adopted in an almost uncritical fashion.

But this convergence has not led to an easy consensus so much as to a new crisis. Leading scholars have raised some very fundamental questions as to how much the historical critical method can really deliver.[8] There is a growing recognition that the underlying principles of such scholarship are themselves faith statements which belong essentially to another faith. Using the historical critical method in relation to the Bible is rather like asking a Marxist to critique the Koran, or a Protestant to critique Catholic tradition. It would not be surprising if the study that emerged did some considerable violence to the documents under review. If one tradition is to critique another, then we have to recognise that the perspectives of that tradition will tend to produce a particular result. That is not to say that the conclusions have no value, but only that they cannot be seen as somehow the only objective perspective possible, with all other views being condemned as somehow subjective (with an implied worthlessness) by contrast.

Restoring the centrality of Scripture. Beeby is addressing an increasingly receptive audience. Whither biblical scholarship? The question is very much under discussion. That does not mean that every question which has been raised about the Bible can now be forgotten. Still less does it mean that we can simply suggest that the Bible resumes its former place as the foundation of public truth in the West and becomes again the inspiration of our culture, quietly forgetting that the last three hundred years ever took place. But it does mean that the Christian community has an opportunity to ask some hard but, hopefully, creative questions concerning the authority of the Bible. Most importantly of all comes that uncomfortable question, 'what does it mean to treat the Bible as Scripture?' Is it the case that even amongst evangelicals the Bible has become something of an icon, something revered and acknowledged, but something which can also be ignored, having paid lip service to the sacred idea of its authority? Has the idea that the Bible is authoritative become more sacred than the pages of Scripture itself?

In order for us to grasp once more the authority of the Bible, it is necessary to move beyond a simple biblicism, or even worse a bibliolatry. The Bible was never intended to be worshipped, but to point to the one who is to be worshipped. Nor is the quest to understand the nature of the authority of the Bible simply an attempt to prop up the failing authority of the church. The task is much more important than that. The need to rediscover the authority of the Bible is essential because false authorities have taken the place of the authority of the Bible. False authority tends to lead humanity towards tragedy. The history of the West in our century has demonstrated what happens when the authority which was formerly attached to the Bible becomes attached to secular myths.[9] The idea that history contains within itself certain inevitable forces which produce a secular version of the Fall and redemption, have proved attractive to thinkers of the extreme political right and left. But the idea that a personal God who loves us can also redeem us in the course of history, is very different from ascribing the same ideas to the impersonal forces of history itself. History cannot love anyone and in truth cannot save anyone.

Concentrating on a naive biblicism which either seeks to accomodate the Bible to the prevailing world-view, or which seeks to defend that which the Bible does not claim, only serves to hide the message of the Bible. Yet it is just that message that our culture needs. It needs it not only because the alternatives are far worse, and not merely because the images contained in the Bible are so attractive and stimulating for our creative imagination, but most of all because the message is true.

It is true that we are loved and created for a purpose. The God who made us has not forgotten us or the universe in which we live. He is in control of our future and that can give us legitimate grounds for hope. The God of the Bible does care for the poor and the downtrodden. Justice and mercy are part of his nature. He has appeared in history to reveal his character. He uses the weak and the foolish to shame those who are strong. The death and resurrection of Jesus upon a cross is a pivotal point from which to understand the story of our world. The church is part of God's purpose to bring dignity, reconciliation, peace and forgiveness to the human condition. These things are true.

From age to age

It is clear that the themes of exploring the content of the message, renewing the community that proclaims it, and recovering the authority for that message, are three sides of the one missionary enterprise. These three ingredients in the missionary agenda all depend upon each other. But in seeking to strengthen the life of those who are to engage in mission there is a danger that the missionary agenda might become too introverted. It is vital to remember that the focus for mission is not the church, but the culture in which the church is set.

Throughout this study there has come the suggestion that the missionaries which the church needs in order to speak to the age which is coming will tend to be dissenters. There is perhaps a fine line between a dissenter and a crank. The church has had its share of cranks. Indeed some would say it has had more than its share! Sometimes it is those who are regarded as awkward misfits who enable the church to live through a time of pressure. The passing from one age to another is inevitably such a time. It has hardly been fashionable for anyone to be identified with the church during our own time. There have been a few exceptions who have lived as Christians and who have also won the admiration of the secular world: Martin Luther King, Mother Theresa and Dietrich Bonhoeffer to name a few. But for the most part, those who have been on the cutting edge of change in contemporary society have not been Christians.

Experiences in Eastern Europe. Those who are part of the Christian community are sensing that a change is coming. Recent years have seen large numbers of converts to Christianity throughout large parts of Eastern Europe. Events in those parts of Europe are felt by many to be a harbinger of the change that might come to the West in the coming decades. It has been possible to identify three very different kinds of people who have featured in that changing scenario.[10]

First, there have been those persecuted individuals who have kept the church alive through years of hardship. Most of those who experienced such pain longed for the day when it would be possible to worship openly, to teach the faith to their children without fear, and to speak freely to their neighbours about the claims of Christ without threat of imprisonment. Strangely, now that such a day has come, many of those who longed for such a new age are puzzled and bewildered by the change. They are not sure what to make of those who now clamour to join the church. The new freedom has sometimes been experienced as an unwelcome change simply because it is so strange.

Secondly, there are those who yearned for an experience of the Christian faith but never embraced it in the dark years of persecution. Many of those have been so numbed by the years of official atheism, that they lack the courage to embrace the new freedoms and to launch out in order to discover faith. Instead, they often bring their children to the church. 'We want you to teach the faith to our children,' they say. 'It is too late for us. We cannot change. The only hope is for our children.'

Thirdly, there are those courageous, imaginative and innovative individuals who are coming to faith. But they are often perplexed by the church that they encounter. They take the message of the Christian gospel seriously and wish to see society radically reshaped in accordance with that message. Such people cannot always be contained by the church which already exists, and they often launch out to create new forms of the church. The survival of the persecuted church depended on those who were misfits in society, but the future of the church lies with those who dare to think differently, not just about society, but also about the church. The growing, vibrant church of Eastern Europe is increasingly led by new converts to the faith.

The new missionary church of the West. The story of the conversion of the British Isles strongly features the life of St Patrick. The defining moment of St Patrick's mission revolves around the lighting of a particular beacon. The story tells of how the High King of Ireland celebrated a pagan feast on the hill of Tara. According to custom, no one was permitted to light a fire before a fire appeared in the palace of Tara. St Patrick decided to celebrate Easter on the plain below the hill of Tara on the night before that feast was held. In order to do this he chose to light a fire on the plain, knowing that it would be observed from the palace. According to the story, the druids told the High King Loegaire that unless St Patrick's fire was extinguished that same night, it would never be put out:

> It will even rise above all the fires of our customs and he who has kindled it on this night will overpower us all and you, and will seduce all the people of your kingdom, and all kingdoms will yield to it, and it will spread over the whole country and will reign in all eternity.[11]

Needless to say, it was not put out and Patrick's beacon burned ever more brightly. The new missionary church of the West seeks those who will have the courage to light a new beacon, one which will illumine the age which is to come.

REFERENCES

Introduction

1. The writer Lesslie Newbigin has recently completed the manuscript for a book entitled, *Proper Confidence*. I have had the privilege of reading this manuscript. It deals with the extent to which all forms of knowing are based ultimately on faith of some kind. He explores the question of the extent to which we might have a 'proper confidence' in what we believe.
2. William Rees-Mogg, in 'Artists of despair: the smell of death has dominated the creative outlook of our tortured age', *The Times*, (17 Feb 1994). p16.

Chapter One

1. The biographer of John Reith describes the correspondence of those who wrote to the BBC complaining of its use in propagating Christian views when such broadcasts first began. See Ian McIntyre, *Expense of Glory: Life of John Reith of the BBC*, HarperCollins. 1993.
2. These figures have been given to me by the compiler of research undertaken by Dawn Denmark and unpublished at the time of writing.
3. Gunnar Hansson (Ed), *Bible Reading in Sweden*, Almqvist & Wiksell, 1990, p23.
4. *The International Review of Mission*, April 1974, p157.
5. This quotation from Pope Paul VI is referred to by Bishop

Crispian Hollis in the Maryvale Lecture published in *Briefing*, 14 October 1993, p10ff

6. Henry Chadwick, *The Early Church*, Pelican, 1967, p288.

7. Os Guinness, *The American Hour*, Free Press, 1993, p4.

8. Found in *The Loss of Virtue: Moral Confusion and Social Disorder in Britain and America*. Digby Anderson (Ed), The Social Affairs Unit, 1992.

9. *Ibid* p237.

10. Kenneth Clark, *Civilisation*, Penguin, 1969, p246.

11. This remark was made by the industrialist James Alcock in a talk entitled *What's Wrong With Our Culture*, London, Feb 1993.

12. Os Guinness, *The American Hour*, Free Press, 1993, p172.

13. Paul Edwards, *The Encyclopedia of Unbelief*, Vol 1, Prometheus Books, 1985, pxiii.

14. Wolfhart Pannenberg highlights this pain in *Christianity in a Secularised World*, SCM, 1988.

15. Paul Tillich, *The Shaking of the Foundation*, Pelican, 1962, p181.

16. Dan Beeby, *Treasure in the Field*, p242.

17. *Ibid* p250.

18. Steve Bruce, *Religion and Modernisation*, Clarendon Press, 1992, p11.

19. This debate is well reflected in the book edited by Steve Bruce, *Religion and Modernisation*, Clarendon Press, 1992.

20. Peter Berger, *A Far Glory*, The Free Press, 1992, p32.

21. This theory is advanced by Wolfhart Pannenberg in *Christianity in a Secularised World*, SCM, 1988.

22. Vishal Mangalwadi, *In Search of Self*, Spire Books, 1992, p25.

23. Wicca is the name usually given to the practice of modern pagan worship. For a presentation of such beliefs see David Burnett, *The Dawning of the Pagan Moon*, Monarch, 1991.

24. Vishal Mangalwadi, *op cit*.

25. For a fuller treatment of this theme see *Winning Hearts, Changing Minds*, Monarch, 2001, previously published as *To Win the West*.

26. The present Prime Minister of Zambia has described his own country in these terms in a number of public speeches.

27. Michael Fanstone, *The Sheep That Got Away*, Monarch, 1993, p22.

28. Mary Midgley, *Science as Religion: A Modern Myth and its Meaning*, Routledge, 1992

29. Vishal Mangalwadi, *op cit*, p270f.

Chapter Two

1. David Burnett, *Clash of Worlds*, Monarch, 1990, pp12-20.

2. Lesslie Newbigin uses this concept in *The Gospel in a Pluralist Society*, SPCK, 1989, see especially p25. It is a concept borrowed from the work of sociologists, in particular from Peter Berger's book *The Rumour of Angels*, Doubleday, 1970.

3. This story was told by former missionary, now teaching missions, John Ball, at the opening address of the British and Irish Association of Mission Studies conference held in Lampeter, 1993.

4. It is important to balance any remarks about Descartes with the comment that Descartes did not invent the idea of doubt so much as he attempted to deal with the problem of doubt which had already emerged as an intellectual debate.

5. Lesslie Newbigin, *Foolishness to the Greeks*, SPCK, 1986, p25.

6. The writer Michael Buckley has made a very detailed study of the thinking of Diderot, Lessius, Rousseau and others which traces their various contributions to atheism and paganism in *At the Origins of Modern Atheism*, Yale University Press, 1987.

7. Psychologists have long debated the question 'Does religion make you ill?' Despite a good deal of statistical evidence to the contrary, there seems to be a bias on the part of psychology and psychiatry that religion must be in some way either an expression of unhealthy tendencies, or something which tends to lead to mental instability. The views of Freud on the place and function of religion form part of this long antipathy towards religion in general.

8. Mary Midgley, *Science as Salvation*, Routledge, 1992, p52.

9. Stephen Hawking, *A Brief History of Time*, Bantam Press, 1988, p13.

10. One of the foremost works on this subject is that by John Milbank, *Theology of Social Theory*, Blackwell, 1992.

11. Lesslie Newbigin, *The Gospel in a Pluralist Society*, SPCK, 1989, p20.

12. *Ibid.*

13. Mary Midgley, *The Gospel and Contemporary Society*, SPCK, 1992, p41.

14. *Ibid.*

15. Lesslie Newbigin, *The Gospel in a Pluralist Society*, SPCK, 1989, p14.

16. *Ibid* pp14–19.

17. *Ibid* p15f.

18. *Ibid* p211.

19. Os Guinness, *The American Hour*, The Free Press, 1993, p348.

20. Fukuyama, *The End of History and the Last Man*, Penguin, 1993.

21. Leslie J. Francis, Harry M. Gibson, Peter Fulljames, 'Attitudes Towards Christianity, Creationism, Scientism and Interest Among 11–15 Year Olds', *British Journal of Education*, September, 1990, pp4 ff.

22. Os Guinness, *The American Hour*, The Free Press, 1993, p413.

23. E. F. Schumacher, *Small is Beautiful*, Abacus, 1973, p10f.

24. *Ibid* p11.

25. Hugh M'Leod, *Religion and Modernisation*, Clarendon Press, 1992, p61.

26. These comments were made to me by a group of students (18–21 year olds) who took a course on Christianity in the mid to late 1980s.

Chapter Three

1. Brian Appleyard, *Times Review*, 25 April 1992, p12.

2. Walter Breuggemann, *Texts Under Negotiation*, Fortress Press, 1993, pp3–6.

3. 'The large, experienced reality faced daily by those with whom we minister is the collapse of the white, male, Western world of colonialism. While that world will continue to make its claim for a very long time, its unchallenged authority and credibility are over and done with... The experience of this collapse is profound, intense and quite concrete. There is a lot of political mileage in rhetoric that

pretends the old system works, but it is a deception. Thus the end of modernity, I propose, is not some remote, intellectual fantasy, but reaches down into the lives of folk like us.' *Ibid* p11.

4. 'What has happened to our civilization which, so recently, was confident that it was the "Coming World Civilization"? There had been, of course, earlier voices warning of the end of western civilization. But these were lone voices, and the message hardly reached the average person. We were confident then, even after the appalling events of the First World War and its aftermath, that the "modern scientific world-view" was a true account of how things are, in contrast to the myths of the uncivilized world, that our science and technology held the key to unlimited progress, that free democratic institutions of the world establish themselves everywhere, and that our mastery over Nature would create a world of well-being for all...Today, in spite of some survivals of the older view, the scene has changed almost completely.' Lesslie Newbigin, *The Other Side of 1984*, The Risk Book Series, World Council of Churches, 1983, p2.

5. Jonathan Sacks, *The Persistence of Faith*, Weidenfeld Paperbacks, 1991, p20.

6. *Ibid* p19.

7. 'Shopping has become an activity to stimulate the imagination and excitement, as the soaring arches of gothic had done for the Middle Ages and the vast, imposing ziggurat had done for the cities of ancient Mesopotamia. The fantasy element is completed by the fact that the mall is covered by a great glass roof, complete with artificial weather. Several malls have not only eternal summer, but a fake dawn and dusk... American consumerism seems to be reaching the logical conclusion of the ideals it holds dear – life in a giant Disneyland of shops, lived under an artificial sun, where any aspects of life not centred around the accumulation and spending of money is considered irrelevant.' Mike Starkey, *Born to Shop*, Monarch, 1989, p76f.

8. This phrase was used in a number of election speeches by the leader of the British Labour party, Harold Wilson during his successful 1963 campaign which ended 13 years of Conservative government.

9. John Milbank, *Theology and Social Theory*, Blackwell, 1990, pp275 and 279.

10. 'Man, swept along by science, is certainly not stripped of his illusions, his childish beliefs, dreams, reveries, uncontrolled passions and myth-making – quite the contrary. In the midst of the stammering and questioning, the irrational is the great refuge against the horrors of systematisation. In our era of mathematics, of science, of rigorous discipline, of exact knowledge and abundant factual information, to "know" something is the abomination of desolation. One must be non-directive, without knowledge, without experience, (that crushes the poor other fellow). A professor must not give a course. An actor must not know his part. A writer must not know what he is writing (one writes in order to know who one is). The film producer must not know the film he is about to produce (as Jeanne Moreau said so well). One must not know how to resolve a social or economic problem (the thing is to leap into the revolutionary furnace without knowing what is going to result from it). One must give oneself over to the creative uncertainty of the happening. (It is not for nothing that I have employed the word "must" throughout, for it is a genuine moral imperative.)' Jacques Ellul, *The New Demons*, The Seabury Press, 1975, p148f.

11. Thomas Kuhn makes the point that scientific discoveries depend critically on the operation of new paradigms which allow new kinds of thinking. There is therefore a question as to whether the new discoveries of physics allowed new paradigms to operate or whether the dawning of new paradigms allowed new discoveries to be made. Whichever is true, it is certainly beyond question that new ways of thinking about the world have replaced earlier mechanistic views of the universe.

12. Rodney Holder, *Nothing But Atoms and Molecules?* Monarch, 1993, p99f.

13. *Ibid* p19.

14. Mary Midgley, *Science as Salvation*, Routledge, 1992, p212.

15. Lesslie Newbigin, *The Gospel in a Pluralist Society*, SPCK, 1989, p33.

16. Visser 't Hooft, 'Evangelism Among Europe's Neo-Pagans', *International Review of Mission*, October 1977, p353.

17. John Milbank, *Theology of Social Theory*, Blackwell, 1992, p280.

18. Visser 't Hooft, 'Evangelism Among Europe's Neo-Pagans', *International Review of Mission*, October 1977, p351.

19. Paul Tillich, 'The Shaking of the Foundations', quoted in John A. T. Robinson, *Honest to God*, SCM, 1963, p54f

20. Visser 't Hooft, 'Evangelism Among Europe's Neo-Pagans', *International Review of Mission*, October 1977, p354.

21. The main headings in the analysis of neo-paganism are taken from Visser 't Hooft, 'Evangelism Among Europe's Neo-Pagans', *International Review of Mission*, October 1977, pp349ff, even though the content is not the same.

22. Jacques Ellul, *The New Demons*, The Seabury Press, 1975, p70f.

23. *Ibid* p64.

24. Lesslie Newbigin, *The Gospel in a Pluralist Society*, SPCK, 1989, p163.

25. Kenneth Clarke, *Civilisation*, Penguin Books, 1969, p190.

26. Jacques Ellul, *op cit* p78.

27. Jacques Ellul, *op cit* p180.

28. W. A. Visser 't Hooft, *op cit* p360.

29. Lesslie Newbigin, *The Other Side of 1984*, The Risk Book Series, World Council of Churches, 1983, p1.

30. Vishal Mangalwadi, *In Search of Self*, Spire, 1992, p29.

31. *Ibid* p109.

32. John Milbank, *Theology and Social Theory*, Blackwell, 1990, p279.

33. This particular phrase attributed to Einstein is quoted by Vishal Mangalwadi, *op cit* p243.

34. John Milbank, *op cit* p278.

35. Vishal Mangalwadi, *op cit* p79f.

36. *Ibid* p80.

37. This phrase is very close to the title of a significant book on secularisation and the church by David Lyon, *The Steeple's Shadow*, SPCK, 1985.

Chapter Four

1. David Burnett, *Dawning of the Pagan Moon*, Marc, 1991, p200.

2. Eileen Barker, *New Religious Movements*, HMSO, 1989, p150.

3. *The Times*, 31 December, 1993, p5.

4. *The Times*, 'Scientists team up to trace disease gene', 31 December, 1993, p9.

5. Jonathan Sacks, *The Persistence of Faith*, Weidenfeld Paperbacks, 1991, p71.

6. *Ibid* p77.

7. Robert Bellah, *The Culture of Unbelief*, The University of California Press, 1971, p39.

8. Jonathan Sacks, *op cit* p36.

9. Michael J. Buckley, *At the Origins of Modern Atheism*, Yale University Press, 1987, p10.

10. *Ibid* p196.

11. Thomas Luckman, *The Culture of Unbelief*, The University of California Press, 1971, p23.

12. Steve Bruce, *Religion and Modernisation*, Clarendon Press, 1992, p6.

13. Roger B. Edrington, *Everyday Men*, Peter Lang, 1987.

14. *Ibid* p62f.

15. *Ibid* p64.

16. *Ibid* p96.

17. *Ibid* p107.

18. *Ibid* p83.

19. *Ibid* p84.

20. *Ibid* p114.

21. *Ibid* p139.

22. This is a phrase which I often heard as a minister working amongst such men in another part of Birmingham at the same time that Roger Edrington's research was conducted.

23. James Palmer, *Crisis in the Gulf*, Independent on Sunday, 13 Jan 1991, p17.

Chapter Five

1. Francis M. Tyrell, *Man: Believer and Unbeliever*, Alba House, 1972, p5.
2. *Ibid* p14.
3. The findings of the European Values Survey are contained in Sheena Ashford and Noel Timms, *What Europe Thinks*, Darmouth, 1992. The introduction tells us that, 'It is based on empirical studies carried out in 1981 and 1990 under the aegis of the European Values Systems Study Group, an independent foundation established in 1977. This research initiative arose from an interest in the extent to which the countries of Western Europe could be said to share a common value system and, later, from a desire to assess the nature of any change in values between 1981 and 1990. See p1.
4. Jonathan Sacks, *The Persistence of Faith*, Weidenfeld Paperbacks, 1991, p1.
5. These figures come from a survey undertaken by Dawn Denmark in 1993.
6. For a definition of Folk religion see Edward Bailey (Ed), *A workbook in Popular Religion*, Pantress Publication, 1986, p3.
7. Rosalie Osmond, *Changing Perspectives*, Darton Longman and Todd, 1993, and a Bible Society in England and Wales survey entitled, *Bible, Church and God*, 1985.
8. Rosalie Osmond, *op cit* pp45-47.
9. *Ibid*.
10. Os Guinness, *The American Hour*, Free Press, 1993, p401.
11. *Ibid* p402.
12. William Leith, 'I Knelt Down and Prayed that God Wouldn't Get Me', *The Independent on Sunday* Review Section, 30 August, 1992.
13. George Hunter III, *How to Reach Secular People*, p23, uses the word 'ignostic'.

Chapter Six

1. Alvin Toffler, *Future Shock* Pan Books, 1973.
2. It is important to remember that Kant's use of the term

'subjective' and the popular usage of the same term are not the same thing. By using this term, Kant was not suggesting that the word subjective infers that this was an inferior or unsure way of knowing. For a helpful recent discussion of Kant and his place in modern philosophy see Roger Scruton, *Modern Philosophy*, Sinclair-Stevenson, 1993.

3. J. Andrew Kirk, *Loosing the Chains*, Hodder and Stoughton, 1992, p53.

4. *Ibid* p51ff.

5. Digby Anderson, *The Loss of Virtue*, The Social Affairs Unit, 1992, p7.

6. Christie Davies, *The Loss of Virtue*, The Social Affairs Unit, 1992, pp10-13.

7. *Ibid*.

8. Rosalie Osmond, *Changing Perspective*, Darton Longman and Todd, 1993, p83.

9. *Ibid* p104.

10. *Ibid* p95.

Chapter Seven

1. Scott Fitzgerald, *The Beautiful and the Damned*, Penguin, 1966, p249.

2. Jacques Ellul, *The New Demons*, The Seabury Press, 1975, p17.

3. This survey was conducted by a Baptist minister, Philip Warburton, and is presently unpublished.

4. Jacques Ellul, *op cit*, p133.

Chapter Eight

1. The theme of societal exhaustion as used by Alexander Solzhenitsyn is dealt with by Tom Boogaant, Vital Mission to the Exhausted West, *Urban Mission*, May 1992, p51f.

2. See *Winning Hearts, Changing Minds*, Monarch, 2001, previously published as *To Win the West*.

3. George Hunter III, *How to Reach Secular People*, Abingdon, 1992, p23.

4. Os Guinness, *The American Hour*, Free Press, 1993, p396.

5. Adrian Hastings, *A History of English Christianity* 1920–1990, SCM, (3rd edition), 1991, p661.

6. Martin Robinson, Du Plessis, PhD Thesis, Birmingham University, 1987.

7. For a study on the house church movement see Andrew Walker, *Restoring the Kingdom*, Hodder & Stoughton, 1985. The phrase, 'third stream' or 'third wave', has been adopted by writers such as John Wimber and Peter Wagner to describe that wave of churches which have emerged out of the charismatic movement which are independent groups of churches, Pentecostal in experience but not in denominational affiliation.

8. French worker-priests, Oscar L Arnal, *Priests in Working Class Blue*, Paulist Press, 1986, p53.

9. Martin Robinson, *Planting Tomorrow's Churches Today*, Monarch, 1992, p31f.

10. Ephesians Chapter Four outlines these five ministry gifts.

11. For an excellent reader introducing the characteristics of youth culture, see Quentin J Schultze, *Dancing in the Dark*, Eerdmans, 1991.

12. Andrew Walker, foreword in the book by William Abrahams, *The Logic of Evangelism*, Hodder & Stoughton, 1989, pvi.

13. Charles Tabor, *Issues of Mission*, Unpublished paper presented to the Christian Theological Fellowship, 23 March 1991, p9.

14. John Finney amongst others argues strongly that more people become Christians as a consequence of personal relationships than by any other means, see John Finney, *Finding Faith Today*, Bible Society, 1996.

15. William Abrahams, *The Logic of Evangelism*, Hodder & Stoughton, 1989, p77.

16. Charles Tabor, *op cit*, pp4f.

17. One whole edition of the *International Review of Mission* was dedicated to a refutation of the Church Growth message of Donald McGavran, which was itself a response to the dedication of an earlier edition of the same publication to the advocacy of such views. One cannot help gaining the impression that the considerable resources of the missions establishment were being deliberately marshalled to deal with a perceived heresy.

18. James Munson, *The Nonconformists*, SPCK, 1991, p290.
19. Charles Kraft on insiders in a culture, *Christianity in Culture*, Orbis, 1979, p360.
20. Vincent Donovan, *Christianity Rediscovered*, SCM, 1982.

Chapter Nine

1. Wolfhart Pannenberg, *Basic Questions in Theology* Vol. Two, SCM, 1971, p201.
2. *Ibid* p208.
3. *Ibid* p216.
4. *Ibid*.
5. Michael Ramsey in his book, *God, Christ and the World*, SCM, 1969, speaks only about the problems that modern man has with experiencing the transcendence of God, but does not speak about problems with immanence. Presumably this is because of his perception that experiencing God as immanent is not really a problem for contemporary society.
6. Michael J. Fuss, 'New Age and Europe – A Challenge for Theology', *Mission Studies*, Vol. VIII, 16 February 1991.
7. *Ibid* p193.
8. *Ibid*.
9. W. A. Visser 't Hooft, 'Evangelism Among Europe's Neo-Pagans', *International Review of Mission*, p350.
10. *Workbook on Popular Religion*, p12 cites Alistair Hardy research.
11. Roger B. Edrington, *Everyday Men*, Peter Lang, 1987, p111.
12. Kenneth Clark, *Civilisation*, Penguin Books, 1969, p244.
13. Conrad Hyers, *The Comic Vision and the Christian Faith*, Pilgrim Press, 1981, p22.
14. *Ibid* p33.
15. *Ibid* p34.
16. *Ibid* p36.
17. *Ibid* p154.
18. Peter Berger, *Rumour of Angels*, Doubleday, 1970.
19. *Crick-Crack Club*, Newsletter, p1.
20. Thomas Boomershine, *Story Journey*, Abingdon Press, 1988, p16.

21. *Ibid* p18.

22. *Ibid*.

23. Martin Robinson, *A World Apart*, Monarch, 1992, explores Willow Creek Community Church as a model for reaching unchurched people on their terms, together with some British models which are offered as examples of a similar process.

24. John Wimber, *Power Evangelism*, Hodder & Stoughton, 1985, p89.

25. The Thomasmass (or Tomasmass in Finnish), is described in more detail in *Winning Hearts, Changing Minds*, Monarch, 2001, previously published as *To Win the West*.

Chapter Ten

1. David Bosch, *Transforming Mission*, Orbis, 1991, p1ff.

2. *Ibid* p181ff.

3. John Stott, *Christian Mission in the Modern World*, IVP, 1976.

4. David Edwards in *Real Jesus: How Much Can We Believe?*, Fount, 1992, argues the opposite case but takes account of the issues that need to be faced.

5. John Milbank, *Theology and Social Theory*, Blackwell, 1990, p278ff.

6. *Ibid* p279ff.

7. Lee Strobel, *Inside the Mind of Unchurched Harry and Mary*, Zondervan, 1993, p44ff.

8. Jon F Leverson, *The Bible: Unexamined Commitments of Criticism*, First Things (New York), Feb 1993, p24ff.

9. J.C. O'Neill, *The Bible's Authority*, T&T Clark, 1991.

10. BFBS research on Eastern Europe, available from the Bible Society, Stonehill Green, Westlea, Swindon SN5 7DG.

11. Alannah Hopkin, *The Living Legend of St Patrick*, Grafton Books, 1989, p42.

BIBLIOGRAPHY

Advances in the Psychology of Religion, L.B.Brown (Ed.), Pergamon Press, (1985).

A Far Glory: The Quest for Faith in an Age of Credulity, Peter Berger, The Free Press, (1992).

A History of English Christianity 1920-1990, Adrian Hastings, 3rd Ed, SCM, (1991).

Angels of Light?: The Challenge of the New Age, Lawrence Osborn, Daybreak, (1992).

At the Origins of Modern Atheism, Michael J. Buckley, Yale University Press, (1987).

Basic Questions in Theology: Vol. Two, Wolfhart Pannenberg, SCM, (1971).

Belief and Unbelief: A Philosophy of Self-Knowledge, Michael Novak, University Press of America, (1986).

Born To Shop, Mike Starkey, Monarch, (1989).

Civilisation, Kenneth Clark, Penguin Books, (1969).

Changing Perspective: Christian Culture and Morals in England Today, Rosalie Osmond, Darton, Longman & Todd, (1993).

Christianity in Culture: A Study in Dynamic Biblical Theologizing in Cross-Cultural Perspective, Charles H. Kraft, Orbis, (1979).

Christianity in the 21st Century: Reflections on the Challenges Ahead, Robert Wuthnow, Oxford University Press, (1993).

Christian Mission in the Modern World, John Stott, IVP, 1976.

Christianity Rediscovered, Vincent Donovan, SCM, 1982.

Clash of Worlds, David Burnett, Monarch, (1990).

Contextualization: Meanings, Methods and Models, David J.

Hesselgrave and Edward Rommen, Apollos, (1989)

Dancing in the Dark: Youth, Popular Culture and the Electronic Media, Quentin J. Schultze *et al*, Eerdmans, (1991).

Dawning of the Pagan Moon: An Investigation into the Rise of Western Paganism, David Burnett, Monarch, (1991).

Dimensions of Belief and Unbelief, John R. Connelly, University Press of America, (1980).

Disarming the Secular Gods: Sharing Your Faith So That People Will Listen, Peter C. Moore, IVP, (1989).

Enemy Territory: The Christian Struggle for the Modern World, Andrew Walker, Hodder and Stoughton, (1987).

Everday Men: Living in a Climate of Unbelief, Roger B. Edrington, Peter Lang, (1987).

Evolution as a Religion: Strange Hopes and Stranger Fears, Mary Midgley, Methuen, (1985).

Faith and Unbelief: Uncertainty and Atheism, Fr. Herwig Arts, The Liturgical Press, (1992).

Family and Citizenship: Values in Contemporary Britain, Noel Timms, Dartmouth, (1992).

Foolishness to the Greeks, by Leslie Newbigin, SPCK, 1986.

God, Christ and the World: A Study in Comtemporary Theology, Arthur Michael Ramsey, SCM, (1969).

Honest to God, John A.T. Robinson, SCM, (1963).

How to Reach Secular People, George Hunter III, Abingdon Press, (1992).

In Search of Self: Beyond the New Age, Vishal Mangalwadi, Spire, (1992).

Inside the Mind of Unchurched Harry and Mary: How to Reach Friends and Family who Avoid God and the Church, Lee Strobel, Zondervan, (1993).

International Social Attitudes: The 10th BSA Report, Roger Jowell, Lindsay Brook and Lizanne Dowds (Eds), Dartmouth, (1993).

Living Faith: Belief and Doubt in a Perilous World, Jacques Ellul, Harper & Row, (1983).

Loosing the Chains: Religion as Opium and Liberation, J. Andrew Kirk, Hodder & Stoughton, (1992).

Man: Believer and Unbeliever, Francis M Tyrrell, Alba House, (1974).

Mission and Meaninglessness: The Good News in a World of Suffering and Disorder, Peter Cotterell, SPCK, (1990)

Modern Drama: From Ibsen to Fugard, Terry Hodgson, B.T. Batsford, (1992).

Money and Power, Jacques Ellul, Marshall Pickering, (1986).

Nothing But Atoms and Molecules?: Probing the Limits of Science, Rodney D. Holder, Monarch, (1993).

Power Evangelism: Signs and Wonders Today, John Wimber with Kevin Springer, Hodder & Stoughton, (1985).

Prayer and Modern Man, Jacques Ellul, The Seabury Press, (1979).

Priests in Working-Class Blue: The History of the Worker-Priests (1943-1954), Oscar L. Arnal, Paulist Press, (1986).

Religion and Modernization: Sociologists and Historians Debate the Secularization Thesis, Steve Bruce (Ed), Clarendon Press, (1992).

Religion and the Media: An Introductory Reader, Chris Arthur, University of Wales Press, (1993).

Religious Pluralism and Unbelief: Studies Critical and Comparative, Ian Hamnett (Ed), Routledge, (1990).

Rumour of Angels, Peter Berger, Doubleday, 1990.

Science as Salvation: A Modern Myth and its Meaning, Mary Midgley, Routledge, (1992).

Small is Beautiful, E F Schumacher, Abacus, (1973).

Story Journey: An Invitation to the Gospel as Storytelling, Thomas E Boomershine, Abingdon Press, (1988).

Testament: Belief in an Age of Unbelief. Faith in an Age of Skepticism, Stan Parmisano, Ave Maria Press, (1991).

Texts Under Negotiation: The Bible and Postmodern Imagination, Walter Breuggemann, Fortress Press, (1993).

The American Hour: A Time of Reckoning and the Once and Future Role of Faith, Os Guinness, The Free Press, (1993).

The Bible's Authority: A Portrait of Thinkers from Lessing to Bultmann, J. C. O'Neill, T & T Clark, (1991).

The British: Their Identity and Their Religion, Daniel Jenkins, SCM, (1975).

The British, Their Religious Beliefs and Practices 1800-1986, Terence Thomas (Ed), Routledge, (1988).

The Comic Vision and the Christian Faith: A Celebration of Life and Laughter, Conrad Hyers, Pilgrim Press, (1981).

The Culture of Unbelief: Studies and Proceedings from the First International Symposium on Belief Held at Rome, March 22-27, 1969, Rocco Caporale and Antonio Grumelli (Eds), The University of California Press, (1971).

The Early Church: The Story of the Emergent Christianity from the Apostolic Age to the Foundation of the Church of Rome, Henry Chadwick, Pelican, (1967).

The Encyclopedia of Unbelief (2 Vols.), Gordon Stein (Ed), Prometheus Books, (1985).

The Gospel and Contemporary Culture, Hugh Montefiore (Ed), SPCK, (1992).

The Gospel in a Pluralist Society, Lesslie Newbigin, SPCK, (1989).

The Idea of the Miraculous: The Challenge to Science and Religion, T C Williams, The MacMillan Press, (1990).

The Living Legend of St. Patrick, Alannah Hopkin, Grafton Books, (1989).

The Logic of Evangelism, William Abraham, Hodder & Stoughton, 1989.

The Loss of Virtue: Moral Confusion and Social Disorder in Britain and America, Digby Anderson (Ed), The Social Affairs Unit, (1992).

The New Demons, Jacques Ellul, The Seabury Press, (1975).

The Nonconformists: In Search of a Lost Culture, James Munson, SPCK, (1991).

The Opening of Vision: Nihilism and the Postmodern Situation, David Michael Levin, Routledge, (1988).

Theology and Social Theory: Beyond Secular Reason, John Milbank, Blackwell, (1990).

The Other Side of 1984: Questions for the Churches, Lesslie Newbigin, The Risk Book Series, World Council of Churches, (1983).

The Persistence of Faith: Religion, Morality and Society in a Secular Age, Jonathan Sacks, Weidenfeld Paperbacks, (1991).

The Steeple's Shadow: On the Myths and Realities of Secularization, David Lyon, SPCK, (1985).

Toward the 21st Century in Christian Mission, James M. Phillips and Robert T. Coote (Eds), Eerdmans, (1993).

Transforming Mission: Paradigm Shifts in the Theology of Mission, David J. Bosch, Orbis, (1991).

Treasure in the Field, David Gillett and Michael Scott-Joynt (Eds), Fount, (1993).

Unearthly Powers: A Christian Perspective on Primal and Folk Religion, David Burnett, Monarch, (1988).

Veritatis Splendor: Encyclical Letter Addressed by the Supreme Pontiff Pope John Paul II to all the Bishops of the Catholic Church Regarding Certain Fundamental Questions of the Church's Moral Teaching, Catholic Truth Society, (1993).

What Europe Thinks: A Study of Western European Values, Sheena Ashford and Noel Timms, Dartmouth, (1992).

What I Believe, Jacques Ellul, Eerdmans, (1989).

Winning Them Back: Tackling the Problem of Nominal Christianity, Eddie Gibbs, Monarch, (1993).

Wisdom Information and Wonder: What is Knowledge For?, Mary Midgley, Routledge, (1989).

20/20 Visions: The Futures of Christianity in Britain, Haddon Wilmer (Ed), SPCK, (1992).